House of Our Queer
Healing, Reframing, and Reclaiming
Your Spiritual Practice

Library of Congress Control Number
2022944674

ISBN
978-1-7373643-1-3

Edited by
Cordelia Eddy

Introduction by
Risa Dickens and Amy Torok

Publication Design by
Ashley Renée King

Illustrations by
Jessi Knox

Published in the United States by
Purple Palm Press, located in Chicago, Illinois.
Founded in Cleveland, Ohio.

Printed in PRC

Purple Palm Press titles are available for purchase
at www.purplepalmpress.com and discounts may
be provided when purchased in quantity for store
orders, events, or for educational purposes.

For more information, please contact
info@purplepalmpress.com

About the Publisher

On October 31st, 1969 two gay rights organizations teamed up to protest The San Francisco Examiner after an anti-gay article was published urging for more police raids at gay bars. They created a picket line, and urged others to join them in condemning the paper's insistence on encouraging violence and outing closeted gay people who were arrested at raids. Employees at the paper retaliated by dumping printer ink over the protesters from their windows.

The protesters stamped their ink-covered hands all over the building, creating a sea of purple handprints. Our name, Purple Palm Press, pays homage to these people for doing everything in their power to create a better life for themselves and the queer people to come after them.

We too are dedicated to making our mark, book by book. We are interested in not only providing context around why queer people are statistically more likely to face certain challenges, but also in providing solutions for how to surpass these challenges. When that is not possible, we want to give love and acceptance for what is. PPP was established in August of 2018 in Cleveland, Ohio by Lou Barrett, a queer with big dreams. In 2021, we moved to Chicago, Illinois. However, place can be a very fluid thing. We all live in the same city and we all live far apart.

We owe so much to all of the publishers who came before us who do truly life-saving work.

Thank you for sticking with us as we continue to grow and create a space for ourselves in the greater publishing community.

You can keep up to date on what we're working on by following the founder on Instagram (@louthebarrett) or us (@purpledpalmpress). Visit our website at www.purplepalmpress.com.

Thank you and happy reading.☺

House of Our Queer is a love letter for queer folks who may have left organized religion but fiercely believe in the importance of carving out spiritual practices and spaces that affirm us, connect us, and help us heal. It's part memoir and part supportive guide for queers who want to reimagine spirituality and root into an understanding of their queerness (and themselves) as divine.

> – Eryn Johnson, she/they,
>   Author of *Moon Sign*

The understanding of the Universe, of God/Gods/Deities, of Spirituality, and of why we are all here is a common theme in the lives of many. Due to the discrimination many LGBT+ people face in their religious upbringings, millions have been forced to question not just why they are here but whether they are wanted and valued as they are. This book brings together the existential wonderings that so many of us have with the affirmations of identity that all people deserve. Whether this brings your spirituality up or back or simply becomes a tool to consider the intersection of religion and self, it will no doubt bring peace to its readers.

> — Dr. Kryss Shane, she/her, LSW, LMSW,
>   *Leading LGBT+ Expert*

Mui offers a beacon of hope to queer and trans people caught in the painful division between spirituality and queer culture. Using examples of how she has reclaimed and redefined her relationship to Catholicism and other spiritual practices she guides the reader to a new possibility: one grounded in inclusivity, queerness, and a connection to the great mysteries of spiritual life. A helpful read for queer people who have been ostracized from or forcibly lost connection to Christian faith.

> — Laura Mae Northrup, she/her, MFT,
>   Author of *Radical Healership: How to Build a Values-Driven Healing Practice in a Profit-Driven World*

House of Our Queer: Healing, Reframing, and Reclaiming Your Spiritual Practice

By Bex Mui

Introduction by Risa Dickens and Amy Torok

Purple Palm Press | Chicago, Illinois

Dedication

To all the queer and trans beings out there.
Thank you for finding this book and engaging
in this journey with me.

✦

This printing was made possible by the generosity
of The Only Stefanie Clark.

Introduction

✳ By Bex Mui

~ We feel like we have souls, whether or not we call them that. Personalities, special spirits, or cosmic energies inside us that elude quantifying eyes. Some of us are born softly into religion with sweet hymns, a light sprinkling of water on our infant heads. Others have it thrust aggressively—prejudice, fear, and shame burning like brimstone, down our throats. So many of us are seeking a new approach to religion, something to believe in that feels true, a spiritual place that our whole selves can call home. In this book, Bex Mui builds that house. She takes a loving, compassionate hand, rests it softly on our shoulders, and guides us in and through the collective creation of a new kind of Church, a new mode of spirituality.

We are driven by a sense of longing in our own work and lives. We've dedicated ourselves to this sense that something is missing. Looking at the anxieties and injustices of the world, we long for a chance to rest in an all-loving embrace. But the church hasn't been that safe space. For women branded Witches, for Indigenous people ripped from their communities and abused, for enslaved people who had their enslavement rationalized by the religion of the colonizer, and for all queer and gender-expansive people taught that who they are is sin, the Church has left us traumatized and alienated from the very possibility of faith. In this uplifting and defiant book, Bex Mui offers a version of what Christena Cleveland, author of *God Is A Black Woman* calls "The Holy No."

No! Colonizers and capitalists don't get to keep the incredible power of spiritual practice to themselves. No. We have every right to see ourselves as holy, to commune with what feels divine, to uplift each other with prayer, and to rest ourselves in hope.

Bex learns and shares a navigation she has spent her life charting: away from a narrow faith defined by external expectations and constraints, and toward something much bigger. Faith in our communities, and faith in our true selves.

Drawing deeply from her own experiences of ministry and activism, alienation and acceptance, Bex Mui tells stories that stitch the personal to the political and weave a way forward for queering the church. She shows how tarot, astrology, meditation, and ancestor worship have emerged as world-building tools for Queer and anti-racist faith communities, and how these can become pieces of a reimagined church. And with this, she offers us all the living promise of a holy homecoming.

Bex says, "I live with my queerness as a gift." And Bex's loud and proud spirit is a gift to us all—a welcoming vision of religion that is, as Bex describes, queerness itself: holding space, moving and bending, changing and encouraging us to change too. Inside this space, we make connections between spiritual organizing and social justice activism, between belief and support, and between faith, community, and mental health.

But beyond dreaming of a better way, Bex provides readers with real, practical spiritual tools, ways of thinking, strategies, and prompts for reframing and reflection that can open our minds, and maybe souls, to new ways of envisioning our relationship with divinity and with ourselves. Calling on Goddess energy and a radical, feminist, anti-capitalist, and solidarity-showing Jesus to cast light, throwing rainbows through stained glass, Bex re-welcomes us to the place we'd been missing.

This book is a baptism wherein Bex asks us to plunge into holy waters, wash away the dirt of trauma and prejudice that the Church has come to represent and emerge, scintillating and cleansed into a new understanding of what it means to live a spiritual life. Queering the tarot, honoring the femme divine of any gender, decolonizing spirituality, and sometimes just being in the moment.

This is *House Of Our Queer*, a QTBIPOC-centered community that Bex created for all of us. A call to prayer and a call to action. A safe place to examine hard questions and craft a philosophy that resonates. A space to reclaim not just the idea of Church, but the Bible itself. Here we find Mary Magdalene, Chani Nicholas and Yoko Ono, Angela Davis, Pema Chödrön, Buddha, and the Moon and we imagine not the last supper, but a first supper. A first of many new traditions that we can build and celebrate together with Bex in the house that she made for us all.

- Risa Dickens and Amy Torok,
   Authors of *Missing Witches: Reclaiming True Histories of Feminist Magic*

Table of Contents

Chapter I

Spiritual Roots

~ I have lived many lives in this one lifetime already. I've called many places home, many people family, and many passions, careers. I've let life take me where it seems to want me to go, and in that space I've learned a lot about myself, and I've come a long way from what I first called home.

That place was a small town just off of Cape Cod in Massachusetts, as east coast as you can get. My father, Mui Siew Mun, as we say in Chinese culture with our sur or family names first, was born and raised in Penang, Malaysia. His father, my grandfather, Mui Chi Yin, was the 9th child of his father's 3rd wife, born in Guangzhou, (Canton) China. My grandfather was sold by his parents when he was nine to work on a rubber plantation in Malaysia. He was freed during World War II by the Japanese, and later married my grandmother, Choon Choy Chun who is also Chinese-Malaysian. As a child, understanding the nuances of my family's dynamic—from southern China to the tropical heat and diversity of Malaysia—was challenging, especially growing up in a small town before Google. I had a pencil sharpener globe's idea about where Malaysia was, had seen the TV special "Big Bird in China," and had an outdated print version of the Encyclopedia Britannica that represented Malaysia with a few small paragraphs and an image of a treehouse and tigers. Of course, my father, the trickster that he is, encouraged this lie by affirming that he had grown up in a treehouse with a pet tiger. It wasn't until college, when I made my first trip to Malaysia and saw the city of Penang firsthand, that I fully realized why my Uncle Siew Loon calls our family "The Den of Liars." More like the "Den of Perpetual Jokesters," but for a young girl trying to learn about her roots and culture on the other side of the world, this evasion of the truth, or propensity for jokes over true oral history, did pose some challenges.

Still, over the years I did learn about Malaysia and my family through my father's stories. He is one of seven siblings, and they all lived together in a house with his parents, his uncle and aunt, their children, and his elders. I used to ask him what it was like to live with so many people. It was strange to imagine such a full house while sitting on a twin bed in my own room with the splatter paint wallpaper he let me pick out, the pink and yellow splatters somehow both matching and clashing with the bright pink carpet that haunts the room to this day. My only sibling, my older sister, had her own room next to mine until high school, at which point she turned the basement into a teen-cave—think Hanson and N*Sync shrines, a small TV of her own, and enough space to roll out the spare foldable bed for sleepovers. My dad told me, without hesitation or much fanfare, that he just slept wherever he could. "Under beds, in the hallway, wherever it was coolest." Malaysia is right on the equator, and is just as hot as it is humid. Living in the four season weather of New England, it was hard to imagine sleeping under a bed to avoid the heat.

My dad came to America for grad school and unlike most of his siblings, who also came to the states for school, he stayed after meeting my mom, Paula. They both worked at a Chinese restaurant, Chuck's China Inn, and, per her request, waited to get married until after my mom finished college. She told me that her friends were sure that no man would wait three years to get married, but my dad was different. They later ended up waiting five years to have their first baby, so they could first experience married life without children, a luxury and a radical idea during the 70's—almost as radical as being an interracial couple in a predominantly white town. This was especially true because anti-East Asian sentiment was widespread after the Vietnam War. My parents don't talk much about those challenges, though I've heard stories about what they were told: *"Marriage is hard enough..."* *"Why don't you marry someone of your own kind?"* Perhaps my parents first modeled for me the idea that "love is love." Regardless, they've been married for over 45 years and have taught me a lot about partnerships.

My mom is Polish and Catholic. Her mom, my Babcie, was born on the family farm in my hometown, and married my Dzjadu, who was also Polish. When they got married, my Babcie's parents gave them a plot of land two towns over and my Dzjadu built a house for them. He was a handy carpenter who also built triple bunk beds for my mom to share with her five other siblings. Three girls, three boys, two triple bunk beds, one room. My Babcie was the only grandparent I had a close relationship with, as both of my grandfathers passed away by the time I was two, and I didn't meet my Grandma until I traveled to Malaysia in college. For most of my life,

Babcie lived in the home my Dzjadu built, two towns over from me. One of my uncles and three of my cousins lived down the street from her. I loved growing up with my cousins, nine of us within playing range, all girls except for the youngest boy.

Like most first generation kids, my parents really wanted my sister and I to be "American." They bought a house near a good school and we did our best to "fit in." The reality is, I spent most of my life being labeled as Chinese. I knew that I had a Babcie instead of a grandma, and that meant great food, religious traditions, and Polish festivals. But we didn't have language for mixed race or biracial identity until college when we studied culture. My mother actually recently told me that upon reading that I was biracial in an article I wrote, her first thought was, "You are not." Then, the truth of it sat in. I may have had a different experience if I grew up in a city, or went to a school that taught us about race and identity. But instead, I grew up feeling oppositional to the whiteness of my small, conservative town. And wow, what a wealthy whiteness. We're talking own-your-own-skis-and-horses-wealthy.

For my entire childhood, it felt like we were *the* Chinese family in our small town. This came with its challenges. I often think about what it must have been like for my dad to be the only Chinese person in his new married family. To have neighbors knock on our door when their cat went missing to ask if he'd eaten it. I remember trying to explain why my snack had beans in it, and why it was sweet instead of salty; why my father had two first names instead of one. Meanwhile, no one tried to use either, choosing instead to refer to him as "Moy," an English approximation of our family name, Mui or "Moo-ee."

I have more intense memories, too, like visiting my sister's classmate in the hospital after he had been chased down and hit by a car for being Chinese/East-Asian. It's a scary thing to learn, at such a young age, that people can target you, and intentionally hurt you and people like you, just for being who you are. This is also a scary truth for too many QTBIPOC (Queer, Trans, Black, Indigenous, People of Color) in our country. Being othered as a child is a heavy experience, whether or not children have the language for it. I grew up already knowing the ugly truth of anti-Chinese hatred that the coronavirus pandemic brought to the surface of the American mainstream.

The one place that I felt like I truly fit in was church. We went to St. Anthony's, the only Catholic church in town. In my town, the church was integral to the community. It wasn't just a stuffy old congregation run by angry, homophobic men. It wasn't just where we went to mass on Sunday and had CCD or Sunday School class. Stationed in the center of town, to me, this church was a true community center, brought to life by the people who engaged with it, the shared calendar we honored and the rituals we returned to each year to mark the passing of time. It was a gathering place, a friendly, smiling place where everyone knew your name. I've always been the kind of person that finds the small town within the big city. I like to have a regular bar, grocery store, climbing gym...I want people to know my name and my order. I want to be able to genuinely ask how people are doing when we interact. For me, that practice started in the church.

Yes, that is a Cheers reference and yes, I am comparing this church to a bar.

My father practices Buddhism as a way of life. He scorns people, including my Grandma, who practice it as a religion and honor the Buddhas as gods. I remember him pointing out with a scrunched face how Grandma would put out offerings and candles for the Buddhas, asking for their blessings with a kitchen altar and a platform at the front of the house. We honored my grandfather as an ancestor while I was growing up, but we didn't pray to him. "You don't need all this," he'd say. "If you need my father, just talk to him. I talk to him all the time." I'll share more about my father later on, but for now, just know that his practice of loving-kindness, his generous spirit, and his sincere desire to make his own father proud, deeply shaped my understanding of spirituality and spiritual ritual.

Although he didn't have a religious practice of his own, my dad was supportive of my mother's desire to raise us Catholic. My dad traveled a lot when I was young and wasn't the primary caregiver for us girls. My mom is the kind of woman who goes to church on weekdays to do readings on top of the Sunday requirement. Growing up, I wanted to be like her. I loved going to church. The teachings I learned there offered a roadmap for navigating life, and gave me actionable steps for how to be "good." Growing up as an anxious baby raised by anxious parents, all of us trying our best to do better than the generation before us, the church provided a fundamental support system. For many folks in my family, and for many friends whose lives fit neatly within their norms, it still does.

Like the little Aries-Capricorn-rising that I am, I wanted to excel at church, and I did it all. At 10, I signed up to be in the church's first-ever group of girl altar servers. Before that, we only had altar boys. This allowed me to be one of the two altar servers present at each mass, who serve as little helpers for the priest. I loved wearing a white robe and a wooden cross, and appreciated having tasks to do that made mass more engaging for me. By high school, I became a young lecturer,

023

and got to recite readings, and later a Eucharistic Minister, which meant that I gave out the body and blood of Christ at mass. At this time, I was also teaching Sunday School to three-year-olds and was the leader of my Youth Ministry group. By that point, I secretly harbored hopes of becoming the first woman to become a priest. I started a Bible study group at my public high school and encouraged my friends to join. I didn't yet know that what worked for me doesn't work for everyone. I truly believed that we were "the way, the true, and the light."

That's conservative Cape Cod for you

I followed this path to a Catholic, all-women's college in New Rochelle, New York, just north of Manhattan. College was eye-opening for me in so many ways. I had spent 18 years going to school with the same 150 people from three surrounding towns. Suddenly, I was living in a real city, and was a 20 minute commuter train away from a city of millions. The College of New Rochelle itself was quite small, 60% commuter, and had just four dorms and one cafeteria. At the time, just a few hundred girls lived on campus. The school grounds were originally built as a convent, and all of the buildings looked like old stone castles. The honors classes I took, like "Feminist Perspectives of Medicine," "Gender and Sexuality," and "Race, Class, and Ethnicity" were held in The Tower.

Every once in a while, I think about how I almost went to the Massachusetts College of Pharmacy and Health Sciences in Boston. For teens in my hometown, Boston was the big city. I easily could have gone to Boston after college, married my high school sweetheart, had a few expected kids, and quietly slept with all of the moms in my "Mommy & Me" classes. Luckily, my spirit guides had other plans for me. I somehow received a letter encouraging me to apply to The College of New Rochelle, which ended up being the only school out of the 13 that I had applied to that was in New York or anywhere beyond an hour away from home for that matter. The letter said that I had missed the deadline, but that I should submit a general application anyway. I was admitted, and, to my amazement, was given a full scholarship from someone I later found out was an anonymous donor. I was off to New York.

My classmates were predominantly people of color and when I arrived on campus, it was the first time I was ever considered white. It was tough to go from feeling othered for not being white to immediately being othered for being white. I was crushed and confused. The few Asian girls on campus didn't give me the time of day, and I began the life-long work of navigating white-passing privilege and biracial identity.

As hard as it was, it taught me some powerful lessons:

025

I. People will always try to tell you what you are
II. Our identities are complex
III. Our lived experiences often don't show up on the surface

Eventually, I found my people, I fell in love, I made it through.

College is also when I first "came out," or, identified and articulated who I already was. Ironically, I had come to the school for the Campus Ministry, but what I found was a liberal lesbian school that centered social justice and feminism.

Go figure.

When I was little, being attracted to other girls came naturally to me. Beginning in kindergarten, I had crushes on my friends. I vividly remember having to sit in the "time out" chair after I was caught snatching back a pair of scissors from another kid who wrongfully stole them from my crush, Katy. I sat in the chair, equally upset that I was in trouble and aware that I had no choice but to come to her gallant defense. In high school, I had quietly hooked up with my best friend—more on this later.

In contrast to my hometown, college was a queer-normed society where 99% of the girls were at least bi-curious. In this space, I leapt at the chance to proclaim my identity and leave heterosexuality and its ill-fitting label behind me, alongside my hometown and my twin bed on that bright pink carpet.

During my first two years of college, I explored these new aspects of my sexual identity and relationships while maintaining my practice of going to church every week. My school's campus ministry was interfaith—something I had never experienced as a child—and I could sense that my professors and friends were pushing me to think more critically and hold more space in my religious devotion. Prior to college, I hadn't understood critical thinking, and never dared apply it to "the way, the true, and the light" of the Catholic Church. Eventually, I shared my sexual identity and opened up to everyone in my life, including my parents. The thing I quickly realized about coming out is that you can't use anything to predict how people will react—age, religion, political views, location—none of these are definitive. I've been both pleasantly surprised and horribly disappointed by people when I've tried to use demographic information to predict their reactions.

A theme I did notice at the time was that the people who followed the Catholic Church most closely were also the people who were the least accepting of me. By my junior year of college, I had not only given up on the church, but had angrily turned against it and its followers. Rejection had ripped a hole in my routines and my community. So I took all of the hurt, pain and disappointment I had, and the distance it had created between me and the people I loved, and threw it right back.

In some ways, I blamed the church because I didn't want to blame my loved ones for not supporting me. On some level, I understood their fear for me and my new, uncharted life. I didn't blame them for their desire to cling to the expected path of husband, children, and church. I knew firsthand how much I myself had believed, and even in my anger, a part of me could see that their rejection was coming from love. They had an idea for their lives, their children, and their afterlife, and they wanted me to have that too. I decided that it wasn't their fault that we were divided; it was the fault of the church for keeping their ideas so narrow, for drawing a line between good and bad and for keeping my friends and I on the "bad" side.

This time in my life is what I call the "pain place." I'll talk about this throughout the book, and the ways that it continues to show up and ways that it might be present for you. While I'm writing here from the future—a queer spiritual organizer who feels a strong connection to practices ranging from moon rituals to altars to *The Gospel of Mary Magdalene*—I never want to minimize the pain place, or the time and work it can take to move through it.

For me, that time was over five years. I carried pain and a strong rejection of religion with me when I graduated from college and moved to Manhattan, and eventually Brooklyn. It was with me when I moved into shared housing in Park Slope, a safe-haven for lesbians and queer people, with housemates that I still consider my "Brooklyn Queer Family," even though we all live scattered across the country now. In the pain place, I was angry and I let myself feel. I wore my anger like armor against the bitter reality of loss as I pursued a career path from teacher to national nonprofit LGBTQ advocate. I armed myself against the pain of rejection with the protection and acceptance of the queer community, and ever so slowly, I began to heal.

Don't get me wrong. I'm still angry about the things I was taught (and wasn't taught) and the misogynistic, racist, homophobic and transphobic way that the Catholic Church and other major religious institutions are run. I'm mad as hell that religious leaders spread messages of hate and that some people use these messages to justify discrimination and violence against people like me and the QTBIPOC I'm in community with. I am angry that the labor often falls on us to undo what we've been taught in order to access our own powerful, intuitive and spiritual selves.

In the pain place, I closed the door, locked the door, buried the key, and walked as far away in the other direction as I could. And yet. And yet. As the years went on, and all that fury had burned up, and I had enough space and distance, I slowly started to realize that you can take the Catholic out of the church, but you can't take the church out of the Catholic.

028

Try as I might to leave, years later, I began to realize that I was still being shaped by my religious upbringing, by my spirituality and beliefs. To my surprise, I realized how much this mattered to me, and the disservice I'd done to myself by pushing away my own spirituality along with the church.

Have you ever gotten out of a really bad breakup thinking, "I'm never dating someone like XX again!" Then, convinced you've broken the cycle, you later start dating someone new, only to find out they're shockingly similar to your ex? Whelp, me and the church have this sort of thing going on.

Me: I'll never pray again!

(later that day)

Me: Please, nature. Don't let it rain.
I need to bike home.

Me: God has failed me. God never existed.
I don't need God.

(that night)

Me: Good night universe. Thank you for
watching over me and keeping me safe today.

After years in the pain place, I entered what I call the
"reframing" or "replacing" stage. I was beginning to peek outside
of the pain. I didn't formally attend a church or join a religious
community, but I did turn to rituals, holidays, and practices
when I needed them. I was out of college, no longer living in a
dorm room or surrounded by classmates, friends, and supportive
teachers on the daily. Turns out, life can be really fucking hard,
and I was in need of more support and guidance than I knew I'd
need when I left the church as an angry 20-year-old student. I
began to shift ever-so-slightly in my thinking, and to crack open
just a glimmer of space for my former spiritual self.

I started to revisit the supports and strategies that I had
leaned on when growing up in a faith community. I noticed
that friends who weren't familiar with religion or didn't have
any spiritual practices often struggled to manage their minds
and thought patterns, and had more trouble grappling with and
just making sense of this homophobic and transphobic world. It
made me think about what I was doing differently and how I was
navigating long-term social justice activism. I realized that my
life was still profoundly shaped by my upbringing in organized
religion, and, surprisingly, that I wasn't angry about it anymore.

But that realization alone wasn't going to bring me back
to the church. I had been swimming in joyful queer community
long enough to know that those were not my people, and that
I wasn't going to follow anyone else's ideas about "the way, the
true, and the light." I did want to have something for me, though,
something more. I call this the "reclaiming" phase.

I started to own the rituals and practices that brought me
joy and lifted me up. I started working for a national LGBTQ

029

advocacy organization and doing social justice work full time. I brought my ministry work to the world but this time I shared "the way, the true, and the light" about queer and trans-inclusive spaces, decolonizing gender, and the need for comprehensive sex education. To this day, I'll admit that the Catholic Church is where I learned activism and community organizing. As I'm known to say with all my past loves, they lost a good one when they lost me.

✦

Coming Out as Queer and Spiritual

As a professional queer and social justice advocate, I've had to wrestle with another form of coming out, this time around spirituality. I had slipped so seamlessly into social justice activism that it felt nearly impossible to return, or to hold space again for my religious or spiritual roots.

a.k.a. social justice ministry/ preaching

I remember going on a long walk on a dark Brooklyn night with my friend DJ. We sipped tea, meandered around the emptyish streets and I told him that I knew that spiritual organizing was waiting for me. I was cautiously, oh-so-cautiously considering it, like wading back into the dating pool after getting my heart eviscerated.

The reclaiming phase of my spiritual journey was bringing me so much life and I wanted to share it with others. But I was afraid. I felt the same pangs of fear and judgement that I had felt when I was beginning to open up about my sexual orientation so many years and a college dorm room ago. I recalled my first rounds of sharing my identity with others, of offering people an expanded version of myself and of admitting to a greater depth of experience. And of watching in sadness when they didn't understand, most often because they didn't share the experience.

This time, I was honestly afraid to talk about something that was so universally "uncool" in my circles and to bring up something positive about a topic so many people were still so wounded by. I also felt protective of my spirituality and practices. I didn't want to bring the world into something that felt so precious to me, or risk dividing myself from the community that had saved me after I left the church, especially at a time when I didn't yet have a new community. It wasn't as if the Catholic Church was going to be there for me if this went south. I felt the fear of rejection looming and I wasn't sure I had the strength to start over again, find a new community, and risk it all a second time.

As you know, since you are reading this book, I eventually braved it. And at the end of the day, none of my worries mattered. I did what I've always done, which is to learn and share, learn and invite others in, move towards knowing myself better and away from being what people want me to be. After everything I'd been through with the Catholic Church, you know damn well I wasn't going to let the fear of "excommunication" from the queer activist community keep me from being me.

So, in the fall of 2019, I decided to go for it and pitched a blog on "Coming Out as Queer and Spiritual" for National Coming Out Day. Seeing it on the screen and out in the world, my truths laid bare, was a reminder of the many phases of "coming out" I've gone through over the years. This time felt scarier because the possibility of rejection lived within my community rather than outside of it.

But I wasn't rejected. I wasn't cast out of social justice circles or ostracized at my job. Not everyone in my life wants to be on this journey with me. I respect that and it doesn't destroy the connection we share. What I have found is that sharing my truth, living authentically, and speaking out about where my mind, body, and heart are at, has helped me to live better, find new connections, and build tighter communities.

✦

Queer Spirituality as Mental Health Support

Once I started, I didn't want to stop. Once I had pulled that thread and realized that spiritual organizing and social justice activism actually worked in relation to each other, I knew it was time to spend my energy at that intersection. The thing is, working in social justice activism and advocacy is a dream—but also a challenge. After five years of national advocacy in constant crisis-management mode, I was burned out in a way that I wasn't even able to name or feel.

I knew that something was missing, and I knew that something was spirituality, ritual, and beliefs.

Untainted by institutional misdirection, spiritual practice can lift us up and help us to recharge. Beyond bubble baths and binge-watching TV, I realized how spirituality—rooted in ritual—can be the self-care that LGBTQ+ activists need to address burnout.

I wanted to explore what was filling me up and share it with my community.

I now see everyday examples of my cherished LGBTQ+ community seeking spirituality by any other name. As someone who was raised within organized religion, I'm aware and weary of seeking emotional or energetic comfort in the absence of a deeper spiritual center. We live in a consumerist society that will sell us spiritual support if we let it. We can easily seek validation from social media likes and spend our money on grounding tools like moon boxes sold to us by huge corporations. In our capitalist and distraction-filled society, we can easily lose sight of what is sacred. We can let businesses sell us, if not our "souls," then our contentment and happiness. Without being aware of where we're seeking our spiritual comfort and joy, or maybe even admitting that desire to ourselves, we can be bribed to turn to these methods of validation and prepackaged ritual again and again. And y'all, I get it. I've done it. I'm still doing it in lots of ways. We all are seeking validation, security, and community. Like all humans, queer and trans folks want to know that we are not alone. We wonder why we're here on this planet, and what our purpose in life is. We want to know, just like everyone else, if we're doing this life thing right.

With time, I started to see that believing in something bigger than myself was actually a form of mental health support. I saw the beauty and room for restoration that is possible when 033 we can admit that we don't have all of the answers. We can ask for support even if we're not exactly sure how or when it'll arrive. And coming together in community can help us to cope and even grow during prolonged times of uncertainty. — See: Pandemic times Is that so scary?

I'm tired of the myth that there is an inherent division between LGBTQ people and religion or spirituality.

Perpetuating this myth alongside disdain and stereotypes of religious people inadvertently supports the hateful messages of the small percentage of conservative religious people who currently drive anti-LGBTQ advocacy. It fuels the myth that LGBTQ people aren't religious or spiritual on our own. To put it simply, they don't own spirituality, faith, or belief, and they can't control our access to these rituals and supports. Feeding into this myth cuts the LGBTQ community off from supports that we actually need, and deserve.

As a person of color and a first-generation American from a double immigrant family, I have inherited generational trauma and hardships that historically have been largely addressed by religion and belief. As a queer person of color, I deserve every strategy available that serves to support my mental health and allows me to feel connected to a greater purpose or some form of higher power or source energy.

As someone who was raised Catholic from a young age, my experience in and interpretation of the world and my presence in it, in this lifetime, has been irrevocably shaped by religion. I no longer see that as a hardship. It is a gift to be able to believe, and in my darkest, hardest, times, it is the most valuable tool I have used to make it through.

035

Chapter II

The Blessing of Queerness

By Bex Mui

~ I live with my queerness as a gift. I'm someone who looked around at the heteronormativity of my small town, with its expectations to grow old, partner off, have some kids, raise them in the same church, until death do you part—and always knew that it wasn't for me. Living outside of heterosexuality was my first experience with giving myself permission to direct my own life, build my own relationships, and figure out who I wanted to be outside of the narrow expectations I was given that never would have worked for me anyway.

Being and living as queer expanded the people I was attracted to and the types of relationships I felt comfortable in. It was the first step I took in understanding that my own intuition, attraction, and desires were what should lead my connections and relationships. Queerness gave me permission to experiment with gender roles and expectations. It also helped me to figure out what type of sexual touch and experiences I wanted to experience. It led me to other possibilities beyond monogamous relationships and connections.

Coming out to my immediate family forced us to recognize that even as the baby of a traditional immigrant family, I was tapping into that "American teen" way. It signaled to my family that I was in charge of directing my own life from that point on. I was making decisions for myself, including who I let into my life and how I was going to live it. As hard as this was, this shift in our family dynamic has served us all well and has given us the space to be both connected and free.

I'm comfortable with my queerness. I dance inside the expansive space that is my queerness, and the queerness of my community. It warms me to be surrounded by and connected to people who are carving their own paths, finding their own joy, and just letting each other be. I've spent over a decade in blissful harmony with my own expansiveness in respect to connections, relationships, and gender. My professional and personal life center around affirming LGBTQ identity, finding joy in queer community and creating chosen family. In my adult life, my queerness has brought me closer to people with shared identities. It has helped me connect with people who share my interests, my understanding of the world, and my vision for family and the future.

Queerness holds space. It moves and bends with us as we grow. It lives outside of mainstream norms and assumptions, and gives us room to be our ever-changing selves, forming ever-evolving emotional, intentional, romantic and/or sexual connections.

When I left the church, it was the queer community that held me and supported me. Queer community celebrated holidays with me, gave me leaders and a history I could see myself in and fueled me with a new mission and purpose. Being cast out from all that I knew was a hell of a transition, pun intended. I felt abandoned by the community that I had done everything I could to be "good" for, emulating the teachings that were all that I knew. And yet, in retrospect, I'm so grateful for my queerness and my ability to listen to myself. Instead of feeling regretful, I have an abundance of appreciation.

Once, during an intuitive energy reading, I was asked, "You're adopted, right?" At first, this really stung. Being mixed race means that I don't exactly look like either of my parents. No one sees me or my sister and says, well, you're a mini Paula or a mini Mui. In fact, growing up, people often thought that my sister and I were twins, even though she's four years older than me, which is a lot for young people. The thing is, we looked more like each other than anyone else, and to most people, that meant "twins!" It also meant that I was asked if I was adopted by many people, especially when they were meeting my parents for the first time. I especially didn't appreciate it showing up in an intuitive reading as an adult.

Before I could crumple into some past pain, the reader said, "Well, you have an adoption mentality." I thought about this. I'm not adopted, so I can't speak for people who are. What I can say, though, is that I have always had an understanding of family and connection that goes beyond feeling connected to people who look just like me. My sister and I were the only Chinese or non-white people in our Polish family growing up. At the same time, when I visit my family in Malaysia, I'm the only half-white, American cousin. Even with my closest biological family, I've always felt a mix of close connection and distance or space.

Maybe that's why I took so easily to building and finding support in my chosen family. I talk about the queer community picking me up when I was rejected by the church. It was the queer community that held me close, loved me, supported me, and validated me. Meanwhile, my family and friends were doing their own work to learn more about me, to unlearn heteronormativity and cisnormativity, and to navigate the religious messages they received that told them to protect—or reject—me at all costs. To me, support isn't merely a vast array of rainbow flags. It is about people—friends, teachers, partners, who are a part of my everyday life, messy and ever-changing as it is, who have loved and accepted me through it all.

To me, chosen family can be a mix of bio and friend family. I don't consider them to be polar opposites. I am blessed with an incredible bio family on both sides, all of whom I'm out to and all of whom I feel a special connection to which ebbs and flows throughout the years. Chosen family are the people who we choose and who choose us. They're people who are learning and growing themselves, and who are open and excited about the ways that we continue to learn and grow. They cheer us on as we try out new ways of expressing ourselves, connecting to others, and figuring out how to do this life thing.

My chosen family is radical, constantly learning, and ever-growing. It consists of people I talk to every day and precious loved ones I haven't seen in years. I left home at 18, have lived in Beijing, China, all around New York City from Westchester to Manhattan to Brooklyn, and now, I'm enjoying calling Oakland, CA home. My chosen family is made up of badass beings from all over the world—Malaysia, Thailand, China, Mexico, Toronto, Hawaii, Austin, Chicago, New York, Boston, Cape Cod(ish) as well as the community I'm proud to know in the Bay Area.

I'm so grateful to be queer, to have had the opportunity to personally define who I want to be in relationships with, and

039

what those relationships look like. I get to determine, outside of norms, who I am and I have found such a fierce chosen family. As scary as it can be to think of branching out beyond your first family, know that there is an abundance of connection to be made in this world, and there is a chosen family waiting to love you, exactly as you are.

✦

Centering
vs. Inclusion

I've always worked within and outside of systems to push for change. When I was a teacher, I also became the "LGBTQ Coordinator," and eventually Diversity Director. My job was to find ways to bring anti-racist LGBTQ supports to our school. I have also organized with the New York Collective of Radical Educators, particularly focusing on their LGBTQ Educator working group. As an LGBTQ and Equity Consultant, I work with people, organizations, and schools to better understand and meet the needs of a wide range of queer and trans folks. Most of this work is with people in power, who are predominantly outside of the LGBTQ+ community and doing their best to understand our experiences in order to change policies and practices. I approach this work as ministry, meeting people and communities where they are, holding space, and giving them the tools, workshops, and resources they need to move towards expansiveness in understanding and concrete actions that can meet our needs. This work complements my spiritual organizing, which is from the community, for the community.

In the reclaiming phase of my journey, I started to really notice the ways that people separated churches from other institutions in our society. As LGBTQ advocates, my colleagues, fellow organizers, and I understand that schools as institutions are places where homophobia and transphobia exist, with leaders that don't create adequate spaces where all students, families, and educators can thrive. This is also true of our country's medical system, government, athletic teams, and so on. In fact, most institutions in our country are plagued by centuries of white supremacy, colonization, puritanical sex-negativity, ableism, homophobia, and transphobia.

And still, most of us continue to participate in these institutions, in our government, our schools, and our medical system. We advocate for them to change, we work within their systems; we still vote, send our kids to school, and go to the doctor when we're sick. Yet, somehow, if a church holds these same principles, we feel like we have some right to demand an explanation. "You went to CHURCH? Aren't you a liberal??"

I remember my first trip back to New York after I had started opening up more about spirituality in my West Coast life. One of my friends was talking about some religious news article and said, "Wait, do some people still pray?" Later, at a housewarming party that night, in a room full of people, someone felt comfortable saying, "Well we're all adults, so I can assume we don't believe in God," like we were in a middle school cafeteria poking fun at Santa Claus believers. Being around people who shared these "universal" ideas blew my mind, especially because liberals tend to otherwise be so very careful about what they say, and put so much effort and energy into not offending people based on language or beliefs—that is, except when it comes to Christianity.

Again, I'm not advocating for Christianity or church leadership here. What I want to pin down is the connection that people make between faith, spirituality and religion, and conservative beliefs, and the harm that can be done when sweeping statements bring these all together. I know, fully in my being, that church leaders and the institutions that they have built have no right to own my spirituality, or monopoly on my ability to seek support from higher powers or source energy. There are LGBTQ-inclusive organizers working within every major reli-

041

gious institution. This work is important and it needs to continue to flourish.

I'm happy when people find or are seeking church communities that are LGBTQ+ affirming. — Not just inclusive For me, it's not enough to be "included" when it comes to spiritual community. Don't get me wrong; I still pause and smile every time I see a church community marching at Pride, and I'm grateful when I see a church with a rainbow flag. — Especially if it's a QTBIPOC flag For me, because of my journey, that isn't enough of a container. I don't want to show up at a space that is not made for me and that's being led by people who haven't lived with the wide capacity for connection and deep and fluid approach to gender expression and roles that we have as a queer community.

The spiritual community I need is one that centers the blessing of queerness, rather than one that celebrates a day or a month of gay.

042

What I'm advocating for is our right as queer people to a spiritual practice. What I'm building is a chance to reimagine spirituality, faith-based communities, and even religion itself, in a way that is rooted in the understanding that LGBTQ+ people are divine beings, living as intended.

⁑

By Us, For Us

I've been an organizer since I was 18, creating brave spaces, affinity groups, and queer community events. After five years of national LGBTQ+ advocacy under a particularly challenging presidency, I realized I was fighting and presenting and working in an unsustainable way that was leaving me depleted, even when fueled by my passion for change. I felt called to balance my advocacy work by creating a space for healing where I worked directly with people within our community to provide spiritual guidance, support, and celebration. I felt that a spiritual practice would be the key for recharging myself as a social activist, and I wanted to spend my time and energy working towards something that would fill me up at the end of the day. I strongly believe in the healing power of queer joy.

By 2020, I was ready to take action. Like I said, Aries-Capricorn-rising, and I need structure. I wanted a religious community again, and this time I wanted one filled with people who understand the deep connection between sexuality and spirituality. I wanted to bring LGBTQ+ folks together to delve into the intersection of queerness, sexuality, and spirituality. I wanted to know what rituals and practices we could co-create if our expansiveness for connection and our deep knowing of ourselves were centered, unfettered by societal norms or even the families we were born into.

043

That's why I started House Of Our Queer, a QTBIPOC-centered community that shares affirmations and spiritual guidance for the queer and trans community. House Of Our Queer honors LGBTQ+ bravery and the skill of looking inward and trusting our own intuitions, our bodies, hearts, and minds to teach us how to build love and connection. We believe that living our truth is the first step we have all taken to awakening our inner spiritual selves. House Of Our Queer honors that we, as LGBTQ+ people, have already felt a calling and have answered it.

I am dreaming up a community of connected LGBTQ+ people interested in spiritual growth where we can learn together, grow together and participate in rituals together without believing in exactly the same things. In fact, a diverse spiritual community where we each have our own beliefs is ideal. Queer Church, where I share weekly offerings and spiritual guidance, is a chance to start anew from a place of curiosity and respect.

✳

My Current
Spiritual Toolbox

I like to think of the spiritual practices that I hold as tools in a toolbox. Each of these ever-evolving practices are different ways for me to access my inner intuition and tap into the abundance of connection and guidance around me that is bigger than myself. Ritual allows me to check in with my life and direct it towards a happier, healthier, and more balanced future, one that is in line with whatever feels like my life purpose at the moment.

Based on the weaving path I have lived, and the winding spiritual journey I have undertaken in this lifetime, my spiritual toolbox currently includes a combination of reimagined Catholic rituals, Buddhist philosophy, queer spiritual practices that incorporate astrology and tarot, and the thread that weaves its way through all of these tools, energy healing work.

I spend afternoons reading *The Gospel of Mary Magdalene*—apostle and goddess of sacred sexuality—and bring a social justice lens to readings of Christianity. I have discovered that the imperfect cis-men who founded the Catholic Church took Jesus' teachings away from his truth as a Middle Eastern, anti-consumerist, radical activist.

I've built new Sunday traditions and rituals timed with the moon's phases. For tougher times, I turn to Buddhist principles. Pema Chödrön's *Living Beautifully: With Uncertainty and Change* is my doctrine. My growing box of tarot, affirmation, and oracle cards invites me to sit quietly for just a moment to make daily pulls. I create tarot spreads for the new and full moon each month, and fuse them with my understanding of the guidance of astrology that extends far beyond sun-sign stereotypes.

Queering Your Spiritual Toolbox, a workshop and presentation that weaves these practices together, is an offering I make for churches, religious organizations, schools and LGBTQ centers. Throughout it all, my goal is to help others find what works for them. One of my favorite jobs is to be a resident "wandering witch" for queer spiritual retreats—think on-hand, just-in-case social worker with more magic, Reiki, and tarot cards. I maintain a "yes, and" mentality to spiritual exploration and spiritual community.

My spiritual self finally feels at home in my queerness. I wish the same for you, dear reader. I'll share more about my winding journey, with offerings along the way. Now, let's explore some strategies to heal, reimagine, and recharge.

What Can You Do?

I. Reflect on Your Blessings in Expansion 045

Have you ever considered your queer or trans-ness a blessing? Try visualizing the world in boxes, and then seeing yourself break, stomp, and bust through by living your authentic truth. You are a divine being, and no true religious leader should try to cut you off from your own intuition because of their own limitations or misinterpretations. That's their journey, not yours.

II. Feel Your Blessing

It's one thing for me to tell you that queerness is a blessing, and another thing for you to believe it. This is a journey and may take some time. That's ok. What does radical expansion feel like to you? What range of things would you wear, what range of connections would you make, if you were guiding yourself? Practice higher-self meditations, and visualize the most authentic version of yourself. What does that person look like? How does that person feel? What does that person need to feel loved? Remember that you always have access to your highest self, and you can always turn to them for guidance or support.

III. Consider Your Own Spiritual Toolbox

I'll share my own journey and give offerings throughout this book for your own spiritual consideration. What practices were you raised with that still bring you comfort? Rather than feeling dissonance if you are interested in or supported by a variety of rituals, beliefs, or communities, can you hold space for yourself and your spiritual journey in multitudes? Does believing one thing necessarily mean you can't believe something else, even if it seems contradictory at first?

IV. Join House Of Our Queer

If you're interested in doing this work together and learning more about where I currently am in my spiritual organizing and offerings, check out: *HouseOfOurQueer.com.*

The Blessing of Queerness

Chapter III

Prayer Reimagined

~ While writing this book it has sometimes felt tough to try to introduce these ideas without feeling like I'm knocking on the doors of queer and trans people who've been harmed, and asking them to sign up for something without first building trust. I was hesitant to put "prayer" in the title of this chapter. Heck, I barely say the word "prayer" to myself anymore. I'd buried the actual idea of prayer so deeply in the "not for me, never again" pile that it took multiple conversations to even admit that that's what this chapter is about.

I am very aware of how willing we are as a queer community to advocate for meditation, but how fearful we are of the idea of prayer. You can't scroll through Instagram without some ad reminding you to breathe or through YouTube without coming across a bunch of five minute meditations. But what would happen if we took those five minutes to breathe and used that time to connect with higher powers, ancestors, spirit guides, or source energy? What would it take for us to give up some of our ego and ask for guidance, to admit to ourselves that we are not wholly in charge of our lives, and recognize that it may not be in our best interest to be? To express gratitude for what we have and ask for guidance in moving forward?

Of course, that's not to say that the benefits of meditation are outside of my practice. Meditation is a valuable mental health support for me when done with intention. It's important to note that meditation is a practice that started in India and has been brought to the United States and adopted throughout the world. Learning more about meditation and breathing can help you build a calming practice that you can always turn to in times of need. This is especially helpful if you're in the pain place around religion, or have recently had to shift your thinking about who and how you call in for support.

049

For me, remembering at times that I am small and surrounded by support has been a mental health strategy that I've truly needed to make it to adulthood. I was taught to pray from such a young age that it became natural for me to turn to a Christian Father-like God in times of need and throughout the day, before bed, before meals, when I heard an ambulance. When I left the Church, one of the greatest losses I experienced was the loss of prayer as a ritual. I felt betrayed by the Church and by the God they had taught me about, which severed this practice, and in turn left me without the support I needed to make it through challenging times.

As I have mentioned, it took years in the pain place to even want to bridge this gap or to reinvent what it means to ask for support for myself through prayer. Over time, however, I started to realize how I had substituted this ritual with a more expansive version that better fit within my world and within my diverse LGBTQ+ community. I had to get back to the roots of prayer and the benefits of feeling small, vulnerable, and held.

I realized that human (cis-male) church leaders and the institutions they built have no right to keep me from participating in a practice that supports my mental health and well-being. They don't own my connection to the higher power they claim for themselves, and, beyond that, there is a wealth of supportive energies and guides that are always there, guiding me.

Building connections with guiding energies, spirit guides and ancestors, and leaning on trust in the universe or the calming beauty of nature has helped me to reclaim this practice for myself. This practice of being still, feeling grounded and held, and calling in for support is something that I can always lean on, and it's there for me even in harder times and in times of pause.

My rituals around calling in for support bring me joy and help me to navigate this challenging world. I feel held when I channel energy from anything that feels bigger than myself, which includes the moon and the stars. While I believe in the benefits and powers of manifesting and have experienced the ways that I can direct my life and curate joy by changing my thinking and perspective, it's also important to balance this with reminding myself that I am not fully in control of my life. I can't direct my life so that I can save myself from pain, so that I can keep things the same when life is in a constant state of change.

I like to call ritual built around calling in for support "spiritual insurance." The thing is, life is unpredictable, and we don't always know when we're going to face a challenge. I've been in therapy since I was 15, and there are definitely stretches of time where I'm not actively working through something. But when I need it, when my Babcie passed away, when my relationship was failing after I'd just made a cross-country relocation or when I realized I needed to leave a job I loved because the working conditions were unsustainable, I was grateful that I had that hour on Tuesday evenings with my therapist, but with myself. I'm a fan of more tools and rituals rather than less. Whether it's therapy, prayer, meditation, or some combination, I make a point to put time into my spiritual insurance for my own well-being. We don't always know when we will need to ask for more support, but building in practices for feeling that connection to higher powers, energies, or ancestors can be there for us when shit hits the fan.

What Can You Do?

I. Choose Your Own Guides

051

To misquote Shakespeare, who I consider a queer ancestor, *"A higher power by any other name would be as sweet."* Do you have moments when you feel in awe of the world? Quiet moments when you can, for a second, feel peace and calm, like things are going to be ok? In those moments, for me, I'm usually at the beach, on a bright sunny day, staring at the vast, expansive ocean. The ocean holds energy that brings me a sense of calm, regardless of what is going on in my life. My love of the ocean is part of my connection to the moon, who pulls the ocean's tides, and is one integral part of my guiding higher power. Whether it's the moon, the universe, nature, a God, Goddess, or Goddex, ancestor, non-binary spirit guide or animal guide, or some combination of these guiding forces, consider where you — even in your mind's eye go to feel at peace and connected to the world around you. Whatever or whoever feels supportive to you at these times, try picturing them, thanking them, or asking to feel held by and connected to them. It is worth noting that no human religious leader owns our access to higher powers. If you've cultivated a relationship with a higher power that no longer feels contained within or connected to a religious institution, know that it is on those leaders and those systems to change. If you want to keep up your practice and connection, go right ahead and do it.

II. Create Mantras

Mantra comes from the Sanskrit word meaning sacred message. I consider mantras to be personal prayer spells. As someone with a very active brain, I do not sit still well. I find it a challenge to access meditation or longer stretches of groundedness and connection that require sitting still. Building mantras into my everyday experience has given me a sense of calm when I've needed it. They also remind me of praying the rosary, which I personally consider a femme practice that allowed me to sit with myself while feeling connected to a higher source. One of my favorite mantras is "Let it be easy." One that I use when working with others is, "This person is doing the best they can with the resources they have." If you're in a challenging spot and finding yourself in a pattern of negative self-talk, connecting to spirit guides and creating your own mantras can be a useful exercise. Mantras can offer a much-needed reminder that we are not alone, and that even the darkest times will pass.

III. Ritual Prayer Spells

Once you figure out and examine who or what you feel comfortable calling in for support, finding consistent times in the day or week to call in for support is a great way to build a practice. We get what we put in when it comes to this exchange. Working at a non-stop job and finding myself being a perpetually over-committed and over-planned individual means I'm more often than not shoving food into my face while I multitask on several screens at once. For me, bringing back prayer before meals has reminded me of the beauty of breaks.

Pausing before my meals to call in for support gives me pause, and reminds me to be grateful for the access I have to fresh food and water. My girlfriend and I have built this into our mealtime practice, and this pause also allows us to take a moment to share our appreciation for each other and our time together before we turn to Netflix.

°53

For me, these words are not just prayers, but spells cast before meals that beam intuition and power into my day. Whether you are starting your morning, having a meal, leaving the house, or taking a shower, I encourage you to try building in some appreciation and connection to the energy and guides around you.

IV. Choose Your Words

One of the barriers for LGBTQ+ folks in calling in for support is the binary way that religious leaders typically think about higher powers.

That is why considering nature and the universe or transcestors can be a useful way to build connection. Typical religious language isn't expansive enough for the incredible depth and breadth of our community. Because of that, I started making and modifying my own prayers from ones that held meaning for me as a child.

From this prayer that I was raised saying before every meal:

> "Bless us, O Lord, and these, Thy gifts, which we are about to receive from Thy bounty. Through Christ, our Lord. Amen."

I created this:

> "Bless us, O Goddesses, for these thy gifts, which we are about to receive. In your mercy, through our own love. Amen."

From The Serenity Prayer, often used at AA meetings:

> "God grant me the serenity to accept the things I cannot change, courage to change the things I can, and the wisdom to know the difference."

I created this:

Queer Serenity Prayer Spell Calling
For Support in Challenging Times

> Higher Powers and Spirit Guides,
> Ancestors, bio family and chosen.

Please guide me through this challenge,
this crossroad, this heaviness.

Help me to awaken my intuition.
My deep inner-knowing.
The patience, comfort, security,
living within me.

Help me to find the serenity
to accept the things I cannot change,
the courage to change the things I can
and the wisdom to know the difference.

Thank you for helping me to ground.
For reminding me in this moment
that I am not alone.

May this prayer spell connect me
to your energy and support,
remind me of my ongoing access to
serenity, courage, and wisdom.

With Thanks

You are not bound by the words or the limitations of the supports around you. If you have or find a mantra, prayer, or God/Goddess that you feel a connection to but isn't expansive enough to meet you where you are, try rewriting or reimagining them for yourself.

V. Honor Your Identity and History

While it's valuable to build our own spiritual toolboxes, rituals, practices, and beliefs, as LGBTQ+ people who were left out or pushed out of many religious institutions and by many religious leaders, we must be mindful and intentional when we build in our own practices. We must consider our race, ability, and privileges as we build. We must name and understand the roots of our chosen practices. I also find that some of our greatest supports as LGBTQ+ spiritual folks can come from expanding and digging deeper into the roots of the cultural and religious practices from our own lineages. Whatever is calling to you, please engage with it with intention, respect, and the time and discipline to research and honor its roots.

Chapter IV Reclaiming Christian Roots, Sacred Sexuality and Honoring the Femme Divine

By Bex Mui

~ I'm not gonna lie, I didn't think there was going to be so much to say in this section. I'd gone through this journey in a subconscious way and hadn't realized all of its intricacies and inner weavings until I actually sat down to write it all out. How hard could it be to approach the deeper roots of Catholicism with some questions, some curiosity, some open-ended exploration, looking to see where it all started? To begin to understand where it had all gone wrong? My cousin Stef once showed me one of those pro-LGBTQ memes, Jesus standing on a ledge, addressing his disciples with "love your neighbor." "But what about homosexuals?" the crowd asks. A blank-faced, clearly frustrated Jesus stares back, "Did I stutter?" I had some idea, some faith even, that if I could get back to the roots of Catholicism, I could make some sort of sense of it all, at least for myself. I had no idea where I'd land two years, a few progressive church sermons, and a whole bunch of banned gospels later.

Starting with
Essential Questions

Like the good English major and former classroom teacher that I am, I started with an essential question. *How?* How did the Catholic Church, and so many institutional Christian churches, end up like this? As a social justice advocate, I've often asked, how did churches or institutions built on spiritual wellness, community well-being, and soul-guidance come to symbolically align—and vocally advocate for conservative beliefs and anti-LGBTQ actions? I couldn't help but wonder why this was the case when everything I could find out about Jesus, who puts the Christ in Christian, showed him to be radical, feminist, anti-capitalist, and solidarity-showing. After all, according to their own Book, Jesus drove out all of the merchants from the temple, asserting that prayer houses weren't to be a "den of robbers" [Matthew 21:12-12]. To me, he doesn't seem like the kind of guy who would be into mega-churches and recurring donation baskets at mass.

By which I mean patriarchal extremes, sex-negativity, shame-as-control, homophobia and transphobia, etc.

059

Overall, everything I've found since I dared to check out Jesus on my own shows that he was a really solid dude. He was the kind of cis-guy who would engage in feminist actions without having to wear a "not all men" t-shirt. He was the kind of guy who would join (or start) an anti-establishment, anti-1% rally without just gassing himself up by incessantly posting about his own actions on every social platform available. He may be the original social justice advocate, leading by example in this whole solidarity thing, taking the time to visit with and listen to marginalized groups ← Read: lepers, women, etc. instead of just deciding what was best for them or having a "white savior" complex. It's worth mentioning that Jesus wasn't white. He was Middle Eastern but has been depicted with progressively lighter skin by white followers over time.

In short, everything that I could find when I was finally in a place to open that door, showed Jesus to be a far cry from the shield he's been made into by the Catholic and evangelical communities. The more I dug deep, the more I found him as a person, spiritual leader, and light worker to be someone with ideals aligned with me and my queer activist community. During Biblical times, women were considered second-class citizens. For this reason, Jesus' love and adoration for Mary Magdalene wasn't merely feminist. It was an act of solidarity and a true subversion of social norms. Everything I could find, in fact, made me confident that Jesus would accept me in all of my truths: radical, queer, femme, lesbian, gender-playful.

As for tackling homophobia and the Bible, this isn't the book for that. Luckily, those books have already been written by Mathew Vines in *God and the Gay Christian* and Daniel Helminiak with *What the Bible Really Says About Homosexuality* alongside so many other works. Not that this makes it any easier when you're in the pain place or if you were raised with homophobic interpretations of the Bible as truth. If you are wrestling with who you are after being taught by some religion or another that you're wrong, or that you should hide, my heart goes out to you. Know that you are not alone, that you are not wrong, and that I am here to encourage you to follow your path and your intuition and to keep loving yourself and creating connections that feel good to you.

Ironically, as connected to and dedicated as I was to the Church while growing up, I didn't ever feel internalized shame for my love of women. I remember having crushes on girls in kindergarten, even being protective of them and enjoying playing with their soft, long hair. It was natural to me. It took me a lot longer to un-learn heteronormativity and realize that I didn't like boys, but that's another story. The thing for me was a loophole about girls in my particular church's teachings. My church was extremely vocal about purity culture and the importance of maintaining virginity until marriage. At 15, I attended "save yourself" retreats where dashing young boys came to tell us about how they were saving themselves for their future wives. One boy gave a speech about how he forgives his fiance even though she "made a mistake" and "lost her purity" by having sex in the past. He claimed to accept her because she repented and since then has waited for him and their marriage. Think "second virginity" here. He went on to discuss at length about how we could be like her, if only we were willing to wait to have sex until marriage. At one such retreat, I wrote letters to my future husband. I would do anything to be able to find them today. I can picture my queer friends and I giggling over the promises I made to my "Dear Future Husband."

The thing is, I heard the message loud and clear and I was all too willing to comply. Don't have sex with boys? Penises are dirty and they ruin your sacred purity and cause diseases and make you pregnant and ruin your future? I KNEW IT. What they didn't mention, not once, was any of the dangers of being with girls. So, when a new girl came to town who became my instant bestie, I didn't have any internal (or external) conflict about turning our sleepovers into something extra. It was my sophomore year of high school, I was in a small town without even the thought of a GSA or Pride. Without having any models for lesbians or queer women, I landed on "it doesn't count, we're just girls."

That isn't to say that my education didn't shape me. I was taught sex ed exclusively by this old-school, small town version of the Catholic Church, save for the one week of high school where a D.A.R.E. officer came to town to scare us about our brains on drugs and our genitals on STIs. I understood, much like the witches in Salem I was learning about, that women are special and our sexuality is powerful. It was easy for me to see Eve as the original witch. She, who strayed from her God-given hetero partner, lured by her subtle polyamorous leanings towards a literal snake, and who thirsted for knowledge and something greater in the world. Of course, she eventually cursed us all. My church never let us forget that Eve's selfishness and infidelity brought evil into the world, and that we as women carried on her curse through the pain of periods and childbirth.

Imagine my surprise and delight, when I heard a reimagined interpretation. In 2019, I started occasionally attending Sunday services again for the first time since college, hoping to answer some of my questions. I didn't want to belong to any one church, but stopping by different places where I wasn't likely to hear anything outright homophobic was a start. It was in a small, modernized service in a monastery in the Berkeley Hills where I heard the homily. The reading was the same, Genesis, the garden, the apple from the forbidden tree of knowledge, and of course, the banishment from Eden. But the interpretation was different. The priest said that it wasn't necessarily a bad thing that Eve had taken the fruit from the tree of knowledge, or that she wanted to share it with Adam. She gave him, and all of us, a choice. What good would humanity be, if we were all born into eternal life and happiness, living in a garden of plenty for our entire lives? What is the point of being good if we haven't actively had to contend with evil?

Of course, I had known that my church was patriarchal. I knew it when I asked my priest why I wouldn't be able to be a priest, and his answer was, "God doesn't want us to know certain things, and he doesn't want us to question them." But until hearing that homily, I hadn't quite realized how limiting the teachings had been around women, how deeply the misogynistic roots went, or the extent to which I still needed healing.

I guess that's why I keep asking essential questions and continue to explore Jesus in my queer spiritual practice. There's always more healing to be done. There's always another layer to uncover. Sometimes I get frustrated by this. My cousin and bestie, Jules, and I often joke that we must have accidentally clicked the "hard route" for this lifetime. Last year, some friends of mine and I—queer women of color—decided that we were done growing and playfully determined 2021 "the year of no growth." But life being as it is, continued growth and change just keeps coming.

We don't have to be completely out of the pain place to plant the seeds of a spiritual practice, to hold some space for belief.

We can do this work in tandem with pain, practicing and healing at the same time. We can do this work knowing that as much as we'd like to be "done," or as close as we might have felt we were to discovering knowing/truth/healing at one point in our lives, we're always starting over. We're always learning, and however annoying it may be, we're always growing too.

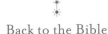

Back to the Bible

"Words are power. And a book is full of words.
Be careful what power you get from it. But know that you do."
—Yoko Ono

My essential questions eventually led me, as an English major, to texts. Or rather, missing texts. Hard as it may be to believe, what we call the Bible is actually just a selection of the recordings of Jesus' words that have been "canonized" or officially recognized by the church. — You know, the church that's been mostly run by cis men for thousands of years?

In schools across the country, we understand as educators that the curriculum we choose for classrooms shapes our understanding of stories, history and beliefs. The people we show as impactful, the events that we focus on or ignore, and the perspectives we highlight are all critical to teaching and learning. Hoping to diversify mandated curriculum is what kept me in an educational consulting job, and has highlighted for so many what we were missing out on without reading books like *An Indigenous Peoples' History of the United States* by Roxanne Dunbar-Ortiz. Books such as these offer new voices, icons, stories, and perspectives, alongside bringing new light to the presumed truths I was taught by the authority figures in my life.

I guess that's why I wasn't truly surprised to be moved by *The Gnostic Gospels* by Elaine Pagels. She outlines how the Emperor Constantine officially "approved" the Christian religion in the year 300, and simultaneously ordered copies of writings that could have been considered the Bible today, to be destroyed. Luckily for us, they weren't destroyed. Rather, they were hidden for almost two thousand years, and discovered in Upper Egypt in 1945. Which is, all things considered, fairly recent. The Gnostic Gospels is generally considered the first popular book on the topic, and it wasn't published until 1979. I'm a Catholic-raised, queer spiritual organizer with a Master's in Literacy, and I didn't even discover it until 2019. It's easy to keep these truths hidden and sometimes it benefits the church for us to stay in the pain place, to reject and to stop asking essential questions.

What I found probably won't surprise you, but if you're like me, I hope it makes you mad as hell. ← no pun intended What was taken out and hidden from the public had a lot to do with autonomy, and far less to do with being a good follower. Further, the canonized text completely erased the gospel written by the only woman—Mary Magdalene. They kept many of the teachings that Jesus gave to his 12 male disciples, but completely erased and re-created the teachings that he gave to his only significant female disciple. What that means is that white, cis, male religious leaders have been editing and filtering Jesus' words and teachings for over 1,700 years. And because we live in a Christian-flavored government, it also means that our policies, laws, and sense of morality are still deeply affected by this decision and the teachings that have stemmed from it. After finding some of the origins of what had gone wrong, I started to imagine what we could do right. What did Jesus say that was so damaging to patriarchal leadership that it was deemed heretical and ordered to be   065 destroyed? What were his teachings to Mary Magdalene? What is the other piece of this puzzle?

Honoring the
Femme Divine

I've always seen the women of the Bible as witches, these powerful women with healing powers. That's especially true of Mary Magdalene, Jesus' femme counterpart, number one disciple, and powerful, nurturing healer. Of course, what I was actually taught growing up was that Mary Magdalene, if mentioned at all, was a worthless sex-worker who was lucky to have Jesus' sympathy in removing all of the seven deadly sins from her dirty body. We were taught that she was special only for being "chosen" to receive his healing, that she existed almost exclusively to demonstrate how holy Jesus was in contrast. The reading was that Jesus was so holy that he was willing to stoop to the level of helping sex workers to bring healing to the people, and that even the lowest of the low could be saved by his guidance, wisdom, and touch.

I've always felt attached to femme power and magick, even in the patriarchal desert that the Catholic Church can be. I know now that honoring the femme divine is a deeply important part of my spiritual practice. I want to be clear that for me, the divine feminine isn't limited to cisgender women or folks fitting into binary and constraining gender roles. I see heteronormativity as limiting, and actively work to decolonize gender and understand the gender binary as a lasting legacy of white supremacist colonization. I do, however, believe in the balance of masc and femme energies, both within us and within partnerships and connections. I do believe that all of us can lean into guidance by or support from a femme divine, regardless of our gender identity or expression. I believe that femme energy has its own magick and I am attuned to it.

Jesus and Mary's relationship has always intrigued me, despite what I was taught about it. Looking back, I realize that part of this came from growing up in a family that adored musicals. If you haven't yet seen *Jesus Christ Superstar*, please put it on your list. I swear, it's like my friend Sunny told me when I was reluctant to watch *Star Wars*, "Just watch it and you'll finally know what everyone is talking about." And if you're not ready or willing to commit to the full hour and 50 minutes, just look up the ballad, "I Don't Know How to Love Him" by Andrew Lloyd Webber. Then imagine me as a young and impressionable queer girl—playing a Catholic good girl—watching and listening on repeat with my family and envisioning my own ideas about love, connection, and the world.

The play focuses on Jesus' last days before his crucifixion and centers around the narrative of Judas, the disciple who ultimately betrayed Jesus and turned him in to the religious authorities. It offered a twist in accounting more of Judas beyond him being a villain/Brutus figure, showing his internal struggles with the decision and the role he was destined to play in history because of it.

Terrence McNally actually takes this a step further in his play *Corpus Christi*, in which he imagines Jesus and Judas as lovers gone wrong, but that's another story.

While my Sunday School classes and homilies at mass continued to sex-shame Mary Magdalene, the musical gave her a voice, compassion, and even a song. "I Don't Know How To Love Him" is essentially an unrequited, one-sided love song where Mary admits to both loving Jesus but also being scared of him and not wanting him to know how she feels because it's so powerful. Think anxious attachment and Britney Spears' "Sometimes" but in the year 33. Beyond the lyrics, though, the play shows their connection, her care for Jesus, and the ways that her femme support and nurtuing made his protests and activism possible.

So who was Mary Magdalene?   067

Was she Jesus' dirty born-again follower, or his right-hand woman? To dig more into this and its consequences and to figure out where Christianity had gone off its rails, I had to learn more, so I went back to the source—*The Gospel of Mary Magdalene*.

Mary Magdalene, Apostle to the Apostles

Personally, I was really invested in the idea that Mary Magdalene had been a sex worker. I'm pro-sex work and sex workers' rights, and appreciated that Jesus chose a sex worker to adore. Sadly, Meggan Watterson, a leading writer and theologian on Mary Magdalene, affirms that one of the only things we know with certainty about Mary Magdalene is that she was not a sex worker. Watterson affirms that the retelling of Jesus' teachings started in the 4th century, when "all gospels that confirmed Mary's spiritual authority and unique relationship with Christ were deemed 'heretical,'" including Mary's Gospel, the only Gospel by a woman, and any scriptures that "confirmed and validated women's leadership in the earliest forms of Christiantiy." Watterson also explains that the widespread rumor that Mary Magdalene was a sex worker was started by Pope Gregory in the 6th century, who started the rumor by mixing her story up with several other sinners in the Bible so as to create a femme fatale archetype.

Essentially, Mary Magdalene was slut-shamed by the church to discredit her, her influence, and her connection to Jesus and to further bury her connection to divine, higher power. Although the Catholic Church officially corrected Gregory's lies in 1969—1,378 years later—I was absolutely still taught this story in the 90s when I was growing up. Mary Magdalene was also only officially "rehabilitated" from her role as "penitent prostitute" to her true significance as "apostle to the apostles" by Pope Francis in 2018. Of course, by 2018, many of us were no longer following the "Pope Weekly" for updates. And, dare I say it's going to take a little more than a condescending "rehabilitation" to right nearly two millennia of slanderous lectures, teachings, rumors, and lies.

It's worth noting that I took some time on this journey to be mad. While it helped me to be academic about these "essential questions" and my exploration of them, the experience nonetheless brought up personal and still-very-real pain. It's not lost on me that the attempted destruction of the truth and misinterpretation of Jesus' teachings has not only caused me pain; it continues to cause pain throughout our country and world—especially for women, femmes and people who have been socialized as women. I needed time to be frustrated and outraged at this type of misogynistic leadership that is present not only in church but throughout all of our institutions. I took some time to scream, cry, throw things, underline, and even walk away at times.

And yet, this uncovered history, these new readings and teachings, offered possibility. They helped me to confirm what I've always felt and known: that something was missing. Important pieces of the puzzle were missing. And those pieces included me, my worth, the worth of my friends, my community, my chosen family. When I was ready to dig in again, I went straight to the now-uncovered sources: *The Gnostic Gospels* and *The Gospel of Mary Magdalene*. I had to learn what Jesus' messages were, unfiltered.

The Gospel of Mary Magdalene

The Gospel of Mary Magdalene, written sometime around the year 100 AD, survived in hiding for over 1500 years. The first copy was discovered in 1896 in Cairo, and wasn't published until 1955. Additionally, not all parts were recovered, including the beginning and four pages in the middle. We'll never truly know all of the messages Jesus relayed to his primary partner, his apostle to the apostles, the first person he returned to after his Resurrection. The messages and teachings that have been uncovered in this gospel, however, form the foundation of my femme divine practice.

A time period which even today, we measure by Jesus' birth

The Gospel of Mary Magdalene, along with other forbidden and hidden texts in The Gnostic Gospels, show Magdalene to be a valued partner, one who stood out and was treated differently from other disciples. My femme divine practice honors that this was not in spite of her being a woman, but because she was a woman, because of her closeness to the magic of femme divine. Because of the depth of holding, nurturing, and withstanding that is possible within our femme sides. The femme that resides in all of us has its own unique and bountiful power and magick, and it is something we can all tap into, regardless of identity or expression.

If you want to read *The Gospel of Mary Magdalene*, you can find it on the internet. But if you really want to study it, I'd check out *Mary Magdalene Revealed* by Meggan Watterson, though warning that her interpretations involve a narrower definition of gender, and definitions of love and relationships that are are more hetero-centered than what works for me. Reading her book, however, helped me to gain a better picture of the magnitude of these secret and special teachings just for Mary.

In the Gospel of Mary, Jesus is sitting with his disciples after he has risen from the dead. I think of this as Jesus giving messages as an enlightened being, someone who has faced his fears and come out on the other side, rather than as the man he was before. According to Karen L. King, this brief but powerful gospel "presents the most straightforward and convincing argument in any early Christian writing for the legitimacy of women's leadership; it offers a sharp critique of illegitimate power" and it asks us to rethink the basis for patriarchal church leadership. Not an insignificant gospel, if you ask me.

Jesus knew that Mary could hear, handle, and preach some of his greatest truths. His messages to her focus on building your inner intuition, on our ability to access the divine through our connection to self, the journey of our spirits after they have left our bodies, and even reimagining the nature of sin. Mary Magdalene is the only one who preaches this. Meanwhile, none of the male disciples can comprehend these deeper truths. Two of the disciples even challenge Magdalene, with Peter going so far as to question her character, finding it impossible to believe that their savior would offer higher teachings to a woman, and accusing her of lying about what she was taught in order to gain status. King also highlights why this and similar texts were deemed so heretical to male church leaders, arguing that their "limited understanding and false pride make it impossible for them to comprehend the truth of the Savior's teaching."

So, even in the year 33, men were upset by femme leadership, by a woman's greater understanding, by a woman who was given that promotion over a man or a group of men. It was all starting to make more sense. We're talking about serious power and control here. Just think of how dangerous it would be to have women thinking that we're more capable of preaching Jesus' teachings than men, or that our bodies and our intuitions are divine. Or how dangerous it would be if we knew that we were chosen and could have been taught those greater truths from Jesus himself.

On Sin

"There is no such thing as sin," said Jesus. (Mary 3:1-3)

I just had to highlight that to start. There's a lot of healing that I've found in *The Gnostic Gospels*, the hidden and buried words of Jesus, and versions of gospels, homilies, and teachings that contradict what I was taught during my traditional Catholic upbringing. This line from the Gospel of Mary truly needs to stand on its own. Reading it wasn't just a healing moment for me, it was a revolution. It was a wave of relief, joy, confusion, anger, and then, understanding.

> *"There is no such thing as sin; rather you yourselves are what produces sin when you act in accordance with the nature of adultery, which is called 'sin.'"* (Mary 3:3-5)

To me, I interpret this "sin" or this thing we call "sin" as when we act out of alignment with ourselves, or rather, our highest selves. Sin itself doesn't exist on its own. It's not a scary monster or devil lurking around to trick people into acting out their dark sides. "Adultery," to me, and for us today, isn't just "sex outside of marriage." We produce sin when we act in accordance with our lowest selves, our selfish selves, our greedy selves. The part of ourselves that disregards boundaries,

071

takes what isn't ours, or acts carelessly or purposefully to hurt others just to get what we want.

Watterson focuses on the a-ha moment of this script in *Mary Magdalene Revealed.* She offers, "Sin in Mary's gospel is not about a long list of moral or religious laws; it's not about wrong action. Sin is simply forgetting the truth and reality of the soul—and then acting from that forgetful state. The body then, the human body, isn't innately sinful." Did you hear that, reader? Our bodies are not sinful. Our bodies are not full of sin. Our bodies are, in fact, divine. And so is our connection to them.

These teachings and messages are so different from the Jesus, son of God, that I had been taught about when I was growing up. As a kid, I was accustomed to walking into churches and homes, seeing a dead Jesus, beaten and bloody, stripped and nailed to plywood, watching over us all. He was both Santa Claus and the boogeyman, watching us while we were sleeping, keeping us in line to make sure we were being good, ready to swoop in with hell fire if we weren't. He was also the father we were born indebted to and ever-hoping to please.

I grew up going to "reconciliation" every six months, a timeline determined by the church. This "confession" was a time for me to share my sins with the priest, who spoke for God. The practice taught me that I was a flawed and sinful little girl, who could be saved or purified by the truth, by my faith, and by my trust in the white cis man on the other side of a stuffy closet. My "penance," or punishment, was always some amount of prayer, Hail Marys or Our Fathers. I'd whisper these in the pew, next to my classmates, kneeling before Jesus' bloody corpse, surrounded by the Stations of the Cross, which was always there to depict the path of torture Jesus took during his final sacrifice.

I'm not saying that it is a negative thing to help kids to reflect on their actions, to tell the truth when they make mistakes, and to build in an understanding that righting wrongs involves work. Again, the roots of the practice have some value. But I can't help but wonder what "reconciliation" would be like if Mary's Gospel were incorporated into the Bible, and perhaps Christian morality, rather than hidden in a cave.

Femme Divine in Sex Ed Advocacy

A big part of my professional life has involved advocating for LGBTQ+ inclusive sexual health, sex ed, and mental health support. People see me, a queer, lesbian, kinky, non-monogamous being, and assume that my work stems from my identity and my desire to help young people receive the education and support that I didn't get as a child. "No child left behind to learn as I have learned! Down with homophobic sex ed!" Of course there is some truth in this. I do want all young people to learn about themselves and have positive relationships with their bodies, their desires, and their connections, wherever they fall on the aromantic to romantic, asexual to allosexual, polyamorous to monogamous spectrums.

Truthfully, however, much of my work involves responding to shame and stigma around sexuality, especially for women, people socialized as women, and anyone whose gender identity or expression is outside of the binary. One of the roots of homophobia in our society stems from deep core beliefs about sexuality that are taught in conservative churches. It breeds from the misogynistic idea that men who choose other men for their partners, bottom for other men, or are feminine in their presentation are "less than" because of their connection to femininity. It breeds from the belief that women who are with other women are "less than" because

073

they lack a male partner. Homophobia thrives at the audacity of women daring to have love, connection, and heaven forbid, sex and pleasure on our own. The stronghold on our bodies that serves to support heteropatriarchy is maintained through shame and control and has lasting effects on us all.

And, in this respect, I'm also talking about reproductive justice here. In part, my spiritual organizing work involves speaking out against sexist and misogynistic conservative Christian beliefs that prevent women and people with uteruses from making critical decisions and receiving the care they deserve for their bodies. As I write this, in 2021, Texas just passed SB 8, the most extreme abortion ban in the country. SB 8 not only bans abortion before most people even know they're pregnant, but it also allows any person, anywhere to sue virtually anyone who acts in support of choice— including providers, abortion funds, and family members acting in support of pregnant people. I won't delve deeply here into pro-choice advocacy, but I have to bring it into this chapter, and this book, because simply daring to reimagine Catholicism and inviting others into this practice implicates me, and I must speak out against the sexist, misogynist, patriarchal and delusional decision-making behind anti-choice legislation.

Read: small groups of conservative, largely white, evangelical Christians

074

What I'll say here is that it is beneficial for conservative church leaders and the maintenance of conservative American societal norms, to control women and people with uteruses, especially in regards to resources that can determine whether we live or die. It benefits them to advocate against comprehensive, pleasure-centered, inclusive sexual health and relationship education. It benefits them to cut all of their followers off from their own bodies, desires, and ability to build powerful communities from intentional connections. It benefits them to shame us out of our autonomy so that we are willing to design our partnerships in ways that they benefit from, like marriage within their establishment, to someone else who belongs to their club, with a promise to raise babies following their teachings.

It is in this way that I have often seen my queerness as a blessing. As an escape. As a portal to another way of being, building community, and finding partnership in this world.

My queerness has always existed and it has taught me to listen to my body and my intuition over the social norms I grew up swimming in, perpetuated by my friends, my family, my school, and my community.

I was ready to learn more about what Jesus had to say in these hidden gospels. What I wasn't expecting to find were indications that Jesus might have been on my side about sacred sexuality.

✤

075

Sacred Sexuality

The truth is, my church growing up was a church of control and church leaders took every opportunity to remind me and my young friends about the ultimate power of sex and female sexuality in particular. Eve, original siren and harlot that she was, tempted Adam with her naked appeal, under the guidance of her polyamorous co-conspirator, ⸺ The devil luring him away from the safety of God's garden.

When I walked into church, there was Jesus, stripped, flogged and beaten, humiliated, and ready to be worshiped. And every Palm Sunday, we were given actual palms and would read out the story of Jesus' crucifixion, coming together as a church community to flog our palms forward and shout, "Crucify him! Crucify him!" This is how I was taught to show devotion through faith.

Of course, my reclaiming of religion has to center reframing and reclaiming sex, sexuality, and desire. Sacred sexuality, for me, encompasses a spiritual connection with my body, a pleasure-centered approach to sexuality, a shame-free exploration of desire, and a firm understanding that sexual connection is one path to raising vibrational frequency, connecting to higher powers, and deepening my intentional connection with others.

That's why House Of Our Queer has had many sexual health advocates and educators featured as spiritual organizers and healers. I knew from the beginning that if I was going to rebuild spirituality for myself and if I was going to draw upon some of my Catholic and Christian roots, that I needed to dedicate time and energy to sacred sexuality and the power that it holds for queer and trans people when we lean in, shed shame and sex-and-kink negativity, and live our truths. That's why I launched Kinky Confessionals. It's a play on reconciliation and an invitation to all to share and release thoughts, fears, desires, and dreams in a shame-free, spiritually-rooted and affirming space. Currently, there's a submission form linked from our Instagram bio where people can send in their anonymous confessions. It serves as a virtual confession portal that is always ready to receive without judgment. Reading people's confessions, sending out energetic support and resources, and sharing affirmations with the community around the importance of honoring our intuitions about desire has been such a joyful part of my work and weekly offerings in Queer Church.

I definitely wasn't expecting to have the power of the body and our connections to others reinforced through digging into the roots of Jesus and Christianity, but there it was. The power of Mary and Jesus' relationship and connection is clear. In her own Gospel, one disciple says to Mary, "Sister, we know the Savior loved you more than all other women. Tell us the words of the Savior that you remember, the things which you know that we don't because we haven't heard them." (Mary 6:1-2).

And it wasn't just that she was Jesus' number one fan. In *The Gnostic Gospels*, Elaine Pagels highlights this text from the Gospel of Phillip: "...the companion of the [Savior is] Mary Magdalene. [But Christ loved] her more than [all] the disciples, and used to kiss her [often] on her mouth."(Gospel of Philip 63.32-64.5). That's right folks. These texts tell the truth of Mary Magdalene, and honor that Jesus both knew and saw her as unique and special, and wasn't ashamed or afraid to bring his body into the connection.

To me, this is also a reminder that Jesus was human. There is a reason he was here as a person on Earth, working with people and communities to help grow and elevate their spirits rather than working magic from above as a god or spirit like his dad. He was sent here, or came here, to do this work from the inside, walking around—just like the rest of us—in a bony sack of flesh. This tells me that Jesus understood that our bodies and the connections we make through them are divine. That our pleasure is divine. That our desire is divine. And he gave this message to Mary, who he chose as his only female disciple, and who he elevated above all twelve of his male disciples. Eve had the courage and the drive to seek knowledge, and made choice central to the human experience. Jesus used power to seek out Mary Magdalene as a preacher and head disciple, teaching her to cultivate her intuition and to embrace connection.

I love reimagining Mary Magdalene and Jesus' relationship. The way I imagine it feels similar to her tender portrayal in *Jesus Christ Superstar*, where Mary holds him and sings, "Don't you know everything's alright, yes everything's fine." I love that her gospel highlights her as someone whose body itself is divine, as someone who can access the divine within her connection to herself (a message that Jesus didn't

pass on to his twelve male disciples). "Be on your guard so that no one deceives you by saying, 'Look over here!' or 'Look over there!' For the child of true Humanity exists within you. Follow it! Those who search for it will find it." [Mary 4:3-7].
Rather than extolling the value of institutional devotion and discipline, his messages to Magdalene were to strengthen her intuition and ability to carve out her own spiritual path.

Sacred sexuality begins with our connection to ourselves and to our own bodies. It also honors the powerful energy that is created through desire, sex and pleasure, whether with yourself or with others. It rejects the idea that we should be disconnected, shamed, or cut off from our bodies, and considers it blasphemous to consider that higher powers would want us walking around numb and cut off from this source of joy. Reading these passages has helped me to reject the sex negativity that was taught to me as a young person, especially having been socialized as a girl. I'm not a chewed piece of gum, losing flavor and vitality as I get "used," as my 8th-grade-science-teacher-turned-sex-educator-for-the-day had so vehemently demonstrated. And I'm not any closer to the fiery pits of hell for engaging in consensual sexual experiences with adults. These truths, unearthed from a banned book, are powerful, and if nothing else remind me that the truths that we seek can't be found in a single text, no matter how sacred it may be.

✺

What Now?

Overall, much of the banned gospels and texts that I could find have centered around Jesus' teachings on building and following our intuitions, honoring our bodies and the value of women as spiritual leaders. By contrast, male leaders at the time focused on devotion, salvation, avoiding sin, being forgiven, and the importance of discipline. What I see in the canonized Bible is what happens when we curate without a diversity lens. What happens when we have part of the puzzle, half of a message, and when we filter that message through like-minded, like-identified leaders. Much like our white and Eurocentric version of history, we have compiled a white, male-centered version of the Christian faith.

My new essential questions focus on balance. What would the world be like if the church had kept all of Jesus' teachings? If parishioners were taught to value their bodies and their intuitions and to stay in alignment with themselves, while also learning the value of ritual and discipline? I've since learned about so many different churches and religious organizations that have been doing this work. Catholics sort of set themselves apart from other Christians. You might think it'd be easy to go on this journey, to give two big middle fingers to the Pope and join a Unitarian Church or some other Christian church with a rainbow flag hanging in front of the building. But it's not that easy.

Decades and so many uncovered truths later, here I am, a queer spiritual organizer and someone who still dares to say that there is value in honoring Catholic roots and rituals. For me, there is value in discipline. There is value in reverence, in ritual. The depths of devotion carved out in me by my Catholic upbringing can't be filled with another Christian church, however accepting it may be. The thing is, the Catholic Church is a family to me. I can complain and be angry, and yet when people outside of the family talk shit about it, I'm like, "You'll never understand!" And so I exist in this in-between space, a familiar place to me as a mix-raced babe, of holding both. But, as I hold on, reimagine, and dare to reclaim, I do so from a new place after this exploration. I hold on while maintaining a deep understanding of the value of going back to the roots, of asking questions and holding space, and of honoring my intuition. Wherever this spiritual journey takes me, ever-evolving as it is, I'll never let that go.

What Can You Do?

I. Build Your Own Sacred Sexuality Practice

We are all walking around in these bodies, these flesh, meat, and bone sacks that carry ourselves around. Especially in a world telling us as women, queer people, and trans people how we should look, how our bodies should be, and controlling what medical interventions we have access to from gender-affirming treatments to birth control, it is a radical act to love, accept, and feel good in our bodies. It is a radical act to allow our bodies to feel shameless pleasure, joy, and connection. For asexual folks, that can mean energetic and intimate connection. For aromantic folks, that can mean sensory play. Sacred sexual practice is rooted in our own bodies, our own connection to self, and our own ability to stir up energy. Second to that is sharing it with others. Queer and trans people have an expansive gift for connecting to our own ever-changing bodies, and sharing that connection with others. Don't be limited by society's expectations. Explore connection for yourself.

II. Know Your Essential Truths

Regardless of whatever any religious institution, leader, or doctrine tries to say, ← Really, whatever anyone tries to say never forget that you, being you, is just right. As long as you're not harming others (non-consensually) and you are acting in alignment with your wants, needs, desires, and true expressions, you are doing what we're meant to be doing in this lifetime. Your true gods, goddesses, and ancestors want this for you.

III. Build Your Own Essential Questions

I hope that sharing my own journey of unpacking and retracing roots has been helpful to you, regardless of your own religious background. Whether you were raised within a belief system or without one, digging into what you were taught, or not taught, and holding essential, guiding questions can be helpful for mental health and clarity. Because of my social justice and literacy background, my essential questions have centered around what went wrong and where these messages came from. You're likely to have questions of your own that can bring you healing. Try writing down some questions or frustrations that you have and remember that questions can lead to new and different wonderings. There's always more to learn.

081

IV. Get to the Root

"Radical simply means 'grasping things at the root.'"
- Angela Davis

In my experience, most religions and spiritual prophets have similar messages for humanity if you get down to the root. For me, this practice helps me to strengthen my own inner intuition, my spiritual compass that doesn't let me down. What is the overall message? What is the most important lesson? Why should we hold these ideas, beliefs, practices? What is the point and what still holds true for us today? If you're looking for some relief from the pain place, getting to the root can be a valuable practice.

V. Consider the Texts

I have read the Bible twice in my life, once as a teen and again in the last few years, while digging into these essential questions. Of course, I'm tired of watching people double down on anti-LGBTQ and misogynistic readings of the Bible. I'm sick of people using the Bible and Jesus to prove how right it is to control women/AFAB people and their bodies and to tell queer and trans people to ignore themselves. There is danger in using text as a weapon, in being too rigid and narrow with interpretations, in using a passage to mean things it doesn't mean and in pulling phrases out of context. I'm highly skeptical of sun sign or astrological chart stereotyping. I'm weary of taking anything that is written as sacred doctrine without passing it by our inner intuition. And yet, that doesn't mean that there is no such thing as a sacred text or that there is no meaning in any of the words of prophets or spiritual leaders throughout history. Find the sacred texts for you, whether they are religious texts, works written by a meaningful author, or powerful quotes from a queer or trancestor.

VI. You're Not Starting From Scratch, and You're Not Alone

One thing that surprised me in this search was discovering just how many churches, religious groups, and non-profit organizations are invested in deconstructing religion, affirming LGBTQ+ people, and working for change. Mathew Vines started The Reformation Project, an organization that creates change and provides learning opportunities for Christian church leaders. Keshet is one of the largest organizations working towards LGBTQ+ equality in Jewish communities. The Queer Muslim Project works on "countering queerphoia and Muslim hate, one story at at time!" LGBTQ+ people exist in every religious community. If you're interested in finding LGBTQ+ folks who share your religious background, whether you're interested in staying connected to your religious heritage or not, remember that you're not alone.

083

VII. Take Your Time

I left the church in a fit of anger, rejection, and disbelief. It was a solid five years before I wanted anything to do with Catholic roots or ritual, and even now, I need some space from people who are practicing without question. Our spirituality, our rituals, our beliefs, these are things that we are here on earth to spend a lifetime working through. Our spiritual paths and journeys are ever-winding, and many of the institutions that direct them are deeply removed from their roots and have a long way to go to be able to meet our community in an authentic way. If you've been harmed, don't pressure yourself to heal. Take the time you need.

Buddhist Practices and Honoring Our Ancestors

Chapter V

By Bex Mui

~ Throughout my life, my parents—my sweet-yet-strong Polish Catholic mom and my strict-yet-silly Buddhist Chinese dad—have always been an example of balance. I'm a being who wants to delve deeply into my passions. I often immerse myself in a belief, subculture, or particular path. And at the same time, being the biracial, mixed kid that I am, I've always been a little in and a little outside of every group, belief, and subculture I dive into.

I've been in and out of groups my whole life, clutching to the railings of a dinghy in threatening waves, somehow keeping a smile on my face. At the end of the day, I'm too freckled to be Chinese, too mixed to be identified, too immigrant to be white, too white to be Chinese, too queer to be Asian, too femme to be masc, too masc to be a lesbian, too lesbian to be queer...

I suppose that's why, even in the depths of my Catholicism and youth ministry leadership, when "the way, the true, and the light" was my mantra, I also always had space for other truths.

I remember during second grade religious education class, a.k.a., "Sunday School," when we talked about hell. I sat in the church basement alongside my peers in a giant metal folding chair around a flimsy table. Meanwhile, the teacher, a parent volunteer, explained how you get to hell and who's going. Going to church on Sundays was mandatory. Knowing that my father fell short of this expectation, she used him as an example. After class, my mother picked me up and I asked her about it, and told her that my teacher said that dad was going to hell. Without hesitation, a breath, or a pause, my mother shook her head, waved her hand dismissively, and told me, "We don't believe that." She explained, using her own ability to use the Bible as a tool for healing and acceptance, that "Jesus says you're either with him or you're against him. Dad isn't against him, so he's with him."

This moment was so burned into my young brain that I can visualize it clearly. Over the years, I have returned to it often, especially during my falling out from the church. It was the first spark of realization that you can build your own beliefs that defy church leadership. Perhaps it's the foundation for what I'm building now, the idea that you can be wholly committed and connected to a spiritual community without needing to think the same way, believe the same things, or follow the same rules.

My father never came to church with us, but it was never lost on me that he didn't need the church to be "good," even in the traditional Christian sense of the word. My mom has always taken note of my father's generosity, the way that he would pay for us, for our family meals, and all the ways he made sure that we were fed, warm, and safe. "Buy it—buy two!" remains his motto. In my lifetime, I've watched him give money to literally every person with a cup or a raised hand we ever passed on the street. I've watched him ferry strangers to their cars with an umbrella when they didn't have one, and was there when he let his own meal grow cold at the Polish festival because he had to make sure the woman that he gave money to understood how to go through the line to get food and had found a place to eat. My father is a good man, without ever having been shamed into it, without having a community of people keeping track of his actions, and without his destiny being held ransom through appeals to an afterlife in heaven. My father's practice of Buddhism as a way of life, as a way of being, as a guiding set of principles to keep oneself accountable, has shaped my spiritual practice and given me a powerful lifeline to lean on when I've needed it most.

Buddhist Connections to Christian Roots: Inner Intuition

When I began writing this book, I had no idea how much Jesus it would contain. My queer friends are probably going to fall out of their chairs at this point. "Not again! We're in the Buddhist chapter!?" Friends, I feel you. Yet, I was surprised to discover that Jesus' hidden messages, formally removed from Christianity in the year 300, hold many philosophical similarities to Buddhist principles. I'll admit, I found this healing. I love learning about the depths of Jesus' messages and imagining what his followers could have done with all of his teachings, with that original balance intact. I'm a social justice advocate, afterall; imagining alternatives to broken systems and uncovering hidden histories is what I do.

The thing is, *The Gospel of Mary Magdalene* offers a "radical interpretation" of Jesus' teachings as a path to "inner spiritual knowledge"(King). Since leaving the church, I never thought that digging into its roots would help this biracial baby meld together the different ways that I was raised to see the world and myself in it. This is probably the reason why this particular strand of digging broke me open so deeply. It is just so different from the lead-and-follow teaching my home church provided. Such a far cry from sit here, kneel now, say this, eat this, drink this, repeat. Inner spiritual knowledge may seem like a basic idea or a fundamental truth to you, but it's truly not the norm. As for me, I'm with King and the other Catholics in camp "radical interpretation." Yet still, it pinged on something that I had been taught by my father. In Buddhist practice and the way that I was raised, the point of life isn't 087 to follow a certain path by completing the right set of steps. I have always been in awe of how my father is just good, already good, because he follows himself and his own intuition.

Pema Chödrön, a queer American nun in the Tibetan Buddhist tradition, is a prolific writer and beloved teacher whose work has been a light for me in some of my most challenging times. She talks about the difference between the Christian, shame-based, weaponized "sin" in contrast to the Buddhist idea of Karma as a teacher:

> "People get into a heavy-duty sin and guilt trip, feeling that if things are going wrong, that means that they did something bad and they are being punished. That's not the idea at all. The idea of karma is that you continually get the teachings that you need to open your heart. To the degree that you didn't understand in the past how to stop protecting your soft spot, how to stop armoring

your heart, you're given this gift of teachings in the
form of your life, to give you everything you need
to open further."

In essence, life helps us to grow through pain. We
experience pain when we are out of alignment with ourselves,
and need to make changes to correct it. As in *The Gospel of Mary
Magdalene*, when we act in ways that we could consider sinful,
the sin isn't a punishment. It's not proof that we are terrible
people, born sinners, flawed beings who need a male priest to
heal and save us. A sin is a lesson and a signal, like pulling the
death card in tarot. It's a painful lesson, and a powerful signal
to ourselves that something is off, that a juncture is coming
whether you're feeling ready for it or not. Sin then invites you
to consider change.

As usual, Pema puts it beautifully:

"Your body and mind intuitively know what's enough.
But in your heart, you have this strong aspiration
that before you die—and hopefully even by next
week—that you'll become more capable of being
open to other people and yourself. The attitude
is one step at a time—four baby steps forward, two
baby steps back. You can just allow it to be like that.
Trust that you have to go at your own speed."

Our bodies, our intuitions, and our ability to connect
to ourselves, this is a critical aspect of my spiritual practice
and beliefs. It is a crucial stepping stone towards truly understanding sacred sexuality as a shame-free, spiritual practice.

The fear of sin and the projected consequences of a fiery,
suffering, afterlife hits home for me, and for other LGBTQ+
folks like me. Loud and aggressive Christians have twisted
the message up, using it incorrectly to keep people like us
from following our intuition. As a young person, it kept me

from sharing who I was, and what I wanted to be, and made it harder for me to imagine myself as an adult. This idea of sin and shame and ignoring our intuition doesn't come from Jesus. And it's not for us to hold onto.

✳

On Death

Anyone who knows me knows that I will talk about death all day. I love talking about things that people hush or try to keep quiet. I'm not only fascinated by morbidity—think bones, tombs, graveyards, taxidermy—but I also have found so much healing in understanding that, like me, many of us are walking around holding unexpressed grief. Like most parts of my identity, I've discovered that talking about and leaning into the hard stuff or the stuff you're taught to hush can actually make it better and lighten it up. We don't need to carry grief or fear of death alone. It's a common, expected, and shared part of all of our lives.

089

The Gospel of Mary Magdalene has helped me to flip my view on death as suffering to death as a natural part of existence. The story actively "rejects Jesus' suffering and death as the path to eternal life"(King). What a revelation and radical interpretation this is! What a far cry from what I was taught as a young Catholic. My church harped so strongly on Jesus' death, his sacrifice, and his suffering. Depicting him bloody and tortured, and making us feel guilty and undeserving. Guilt and suffering were common themes in my Catholic upbringing. The story of Jesus' suffering was used as a way to remind me and the other parishioners that we began life in debt to Jesus and that we would spend our lives trying to make it up to him. But that's not how this story is depicted in Mary Magdalene's gospel. And it's not how it would be treated with a Buddhist mindset, either. Buddhists wouldn't have made an example out of Jesus like my church and so many conservative

Christian churches and organizations have done. Though, Buddhists do regularly address death, passing on, and the arcs of our lifetimes.

I've always been fascinated with the veil between the living and the dead. And my parents have always had a realistic and open dialogue with me about mortality. I was brought to wakes as a young child and knew by age six that my parents wanted to be cremated, not buried. My father used to think that he would die at age 60 like his father did, and often said he was dying when we were growing up. We'd even play at this, he'd call out as if he had a heart attack, lay down unmoving on the floor, only to come to life when I wasn't expecting it— just for a fright. Maybe that seems intense to people who keep death on a shelf that we don't touch... that is, until it finds us. But for me, I grew up learning about, studying, and seeing Jesus' death on repeat from my baptism until high school graduation, so it never phased me.

I gain comfort from the Buddhist principles for life and death as described in Thich Nhat Hanh's *No Death, No Fear: Comforting Wisdom for Life*. In this book, Thich Nhat Hanh considers our earthly lifetime as part of our larger, continual, spiritual evolution across lifetimes. The text also considers our existence in connection to all living things. In my energy work, I engage with past-life readings and the insights that these can bring to our current lives. That may all sound too fluff for you, and that's totally fine. American culture, beautiful in its diversity, does not have one national shared understanding of or cultural ritual around death. People exist on a wide spectrum of connection to and paralyzing fear of death and dying.

The thing is, I have lost a lot of loved ones in my short lifetime. I've lost my first love/first girlfriend, close child-hood friends, family members, and far too many queer and trans youth I've worked with over the years. Then, both of my beloved grandmothers and family matriarchs passed away in 2020, during the COVID-19 outbreak. Death has not been a stranger to me in this lifetime. I have mourned and cried and been filled with rage and grief over these losses. Human that I am, I lean in and do my best to let myself feel when I need to.

And then, when I'm ready, I lean on rituals, and Buddhist principles that bring me comfort and peace. For me, the Buddhist principle that we are causing ourselves pain by knowing a little bit, but not enough, about the end of our lives, rings true. My favorite metaphor from Thich Nhat Hanh centers around the ocean. He says that our lifetimes are like waves in the ocean. You can watch a wave emerge, peak, and crash. You can feel sadness and mourn the loss of that action. And yet, at the same time, that wave was always water, and its crash simply returns it to the ocean that it was always a part of to begin with.

091

Honoring Our Ancestors

I grew up with an altar for my grandfather, Mui Chi Yin, in my home. The only picture we had of him, a small, square, black and white photograph, stood framed next to some offerings—such as porcelain statues and flowers—on a high bookcase overlooking our kitchen. A fitting location for the former restaurant-owner and praised chef. Every October, celebrating the anniversary of his death, we would move his altar to the dining room table. We would bring him tea, peanuts, clementines, and other treats throughout the month, placing them on a red placemat. My favorite tradition was hearing the stories that my father would tell about him, at least one new story each year. Over the years, I've learned so much about my grandfather, despite never meeting him in this lifetime, as he passed away before I was born. I have built a sincere connection to his spirit through my father's devotion and love.

My father doesn't believe in Gods or higher powers in the way that the Catholic side of my family does. He talks to his parents in the spirit world the same way that he would talk to them if they were here. When he sees them in the background of our video chats on my altar, he waves, "Hi mom! Hi dad!" He mourns and feels their loss, and he also knows that they are with him, and with our family at the same time.

Every morning, when I wake up, I go into my office, say good morning to my fish and feed them. I carefully tap on the water to let them know that it's time and then drop their food, pellet by pellet, so they can partake in a little meal-time scavenger hunt on the surface. They are my tiny beautiful light beings—moving around the energy and chi in my home. Then I go to my altar. Cradled in the middle of my bookcase, my altar is at the perfect height for me to stare at the pictures head-on. I say good morning and greet my grandparents. I light incense for them, bow to them, and thank them for watching over me. If I have something coming up that day that I'm nervous or excited about, I tell them. When I'm having a tough time, I tell them.

Choon Choy Chun, my paternal grandmother, lives on a gold stand next to the only picture I've ever had of my grandfather. I took a picture of the picture in my family altar and made it my own. Next to my grandparents, I keep gold coins, haw flakes, peanut candy, and a small statue of Singapore's famous merlion. A picture of my grandma with her children hangs above them. Next to them, I have a porcelain crane incense holder that I light every morning with new incense, while thanking my grandparents for their guidance, and asking for their support throughout the day. At times, I bring this incense around the perimeter of my room to keep their energy flowing through the space.

The picture of my Babcie is a younger one, from when she was about 60 and visited San Francisco. A giant blown-up version of the same picture hung in her home while we were growing up, and it reminds me of how happy she was to be on the West Coast, where I live now. I chose a rose gold braided frame for her, which brings her metallic shine to the altar. She likes sweets and water as offerings.

My Dzjadu's picture is a strange story. It found me when my altar was just for my other grandfather, when my grandmothers still lived in this world. I was unpacking boxes when I first arrived in Oakland, and there it was, a black and white photograph of my grandfather in an army uniform, and an empty, matching frame. I had never seen it before and decided it was time to add him. Strangely enough, when I showed the altar to my family, months later, they were all shocked by the picture. None of them had ever seen it, and most of them had barely seen any pictures of him in the army or from World War II, which he was very private about. I've since added his prayer card for balance. Around Babcie and Dzjadu, I have my purple rosary, some holy water, and a picture of them together when they were young.

My altar always changes. I tend to it like a garden and it grows and shifts over time. I add water, new treats and sweets, and charged stones or other trinkets. I charge offerings by the full moon, with rituals, or in other high-energy spaces in my office, and switch them out to keep the energy of my altar as high frequency as possible. This practice and ritual brings me joy, reminds me that I am connected to my ancestors, and forces me to slow down as I start my day. Like a Zen garden or a Buddha board, these rituals and practices bring mindfulness into my daily routine, and if nothing else, ensure that I don't just roll out of bed, clamor to my work-from-home-station and answer emails first thing every morning.

✦

Finding Your
True Ancestors

I am extremely lucky to have a positive relationship with my biological ancestors and grandparents. I know that this is not the case for everyone in the LGTBQ+ community and that it is also related to privilege and other identities. I was out to both of my grandmothers before they passed away, and having the honor of them truly knowing and loving me, as challenging as it was to share my truth, is a gift. They knew and spent time with girlfriends and sweeties of mine, and moved through their own processes of understanding and coming to accept the whole me. I maintained a loving relationship with each of them throughout their time on this earth. I don't take this for granted. I was especially terrified to come out to my Babcie, a Catholic woman born in 1926 who had lived near me throughout all of my childhood. When I called her to "come out" or bring her in, all sweating with a drum beat in my chest, her response both charmed me and put things in perspective. She told me, "Well, that's surprising, but we came to this country for choices, and if that's your choice, you should be happy." While I know that sexual orientation is not a choice, I love the idea that even if it were a choice and I were choosing it, my Babcie would still support me.

Know that your true ancestors delight when you are living your truth as your authentic self. Biological families and our relationships with them can be challenging. Our parents, grandparents, and ancestors likely did not grow up in a world with as much information and understanding about the nuances of sexual orientation, partnership and connection styles, or expansive notions about gender identity and expression. If your bio family doesn't accept and support you, know that this is their work to do in this lifetime. It's not work that you can do for them, and it's not your responsibility.

Living your truth as an out LGBTQ+ person is a gift to them, a lesson for them about space, diversity, and freedom of being that is increasingly becoming accepted and even protected in parts of the world.

Note
Of course, the ability to live out our identities safely is affected by intersectionality. It's important to acknowledge that Black trans women face the most hostility and are most at risk for hate crimes in our country.

If bio family isn't a part of your support system, I encourage you to build familial connection to queer and trancestors who have paved the way for us today. It's entirely possible that your true ancestors in this lifetime aren't biologically related to you. That's perfectly valid. As members of the queer and trans lineage, we have ancestors dating throughout human history, elders who have paved the way for us to live the lives we are living now, who we can learn from and receive guidance from. We can honor and ask for support from these LGBTQ+ elders and call on them in our ancestral healing.

I consider Marsha P. Johnson to be a queer ancestor. She talks about the making of history, explaining that history isn't simply something you look back upon and say was inevitable. "It happens because people make decisions that are sometimes very impulsive and of the moment." History is those moments, those cumulative realities. Those brave and impulsive moments when we decide to act. I believe that those moments are when we honor our intuition and what we truly want. When we say what we've been keeping silent. When we interrupt instead of holding back and letting assumptions play out. It's when we show up at a family gathering with our partners, regardless of their genders.

095

Remember that you are the next ancestor in your family. The decisions you make in this lifetime are paving the way for those in your lineage that come after you. What patterns do you want to break? What truths do you want to bring into communication? What depth can you breathe into when considering your lineage? What history can you make today?

What Can You Do?

I. Explore Your Lineage

Although at times it has felt challenging, I've benefited so much from being biracial. Having two worlds and more than one culture has helped me to build my own spiritual toolbox that includes a variety of beliefs, practices, and rituals. Digging into the Catholic roots of my Polish immigrant family and the ways that they relied on and were comforted by religion when they needed it most has offered me something very different from exploring my own Catholic upbringing and the space I personally hold for Catholic roots today. What does your lineage hold for you? What religious beliefs or ways of life are rooted in your families or family lineage? Finding out more about where your ancestors came from and went and what part of your family's journey you are a part of can pave the way for your own spiritual journey in this lifetime.

◊ I believe that many queer and trans people are here in this lifetime to break trauma patterns that have existed in families for generations. While challenging, it can be incredibly powerful for our healing to be open to knowing more about where we come from and the rituals that our ancestors have held over time. Having openness towards exploring our heritage in regards to faith and belief, however challenging, can be incredibly powerful for our healing.

II. Explore the Ancestors For You

Never forget that your true ancestors delight when you live in alignment with yourself. Look into the diverse LGBTQ+ history, and find ancestors who share similar identities and affinities to you. Which queer and trancestors speak to you, inspire you, or have paved the way for you to be you? Whose words or actions have inspired your own spiritual growth? How did these ancestors wrestle with their identities and ultimately choose to follow their intuition to live authentically? What could cultivating a relationship with these ancestors bring to your life?

III. Build Your Own Sacred Sexuality Practice

It's worth noting that some of us don't know anything about our biological ancestors. My grandparents are as far back as I can trace in my biological families, and even that is a luxury. I swim between chosen and bio family, and have a strong belief that both can be valuable to our lives and growth. If you're seeking answers or feel called to explore your lineage beyond what you know about your bio family, or if you don't have any current connections to them, you may want to seek out genealogy or DNA tests. Or your path might involve following cultural lineage and exploring the faith and ritual practices within the family that you know. However you explore ancestral paths, know that it's an ongoing journey that is for you and your own self-discovery and healing. Trust yourself and your intuition to lead you to what feels resonant, uplifting, and supportive.

IV. Read Pema Chödrön

I was first introduced to the wisdom of Pema through the LGBTQ+ community, from my radical justice friends in New York. *The Pocket Pema Chödrön* holds little snippets, stories, and offerings that I would read every night before bed. It was the first time I had engaged with spiritual guidance through text outside of the Catholic Church. It offered a familiar practice and a beautifully open, non-judgmental, and realistic view on life, on challenges, and on being honest with ourselves. Pema's works have found their way into my life and the lives of friends around me during some of our toughest times. While I caution folks about delving too deeply into Buddhist practices if it's not a part of your lineage, I consider Pema to be a queer spiritual leader, someone who we can all turn to in times of need.

Note

If Buddhism and its practices speak to your soul, yet fall outside of your cultural lineage and ancestors, it may be a part of your spiritual journey. Engage with caution and care, learn from communities that are culturally and ancestrally connected, and be mindful of the space you take up in community or rituals.

V. Make an Altar

Altars, similar to gravesites or places of worship, are specific, concentrated locations for us to direct our energy during rituals. They are created by the intention with which we tend to them, and in essence, we get out what we put in. Having an altar in your home is one way to remind you to tend to your spiritual garden. Including ancestors in your altar is a reminder that you are surrounded by support, that your life is a continuation of the lives of your families, and that you are never alone. Have fun with your altar. Note how it changes over time, and spend some time each day practicing gratitude towards the ancestral guidance you know is around you, even if you can't see it.

099

VI. Build in Ancestor Routines

Altars are just one way to connect with our ancestors. There are many ways to remember that we are part of a longer lineage, and to call in for support by connecting to those who came before us—those who are waiting and watching for us to spiritually wake up, live our truths, and move through the world authentically. Find a sacred place or a place that can become sacred to you, perhaps somewhere that your ancestors went and enjoyed, a place where you can connect to them. We don't always have to be solemn and chaste when we engage in ritual work. While we need intention in our practices, we can connect to our ancestors through dance, laughter, and good food. I co-host a monthly QTBIPOC potluck, centered around the food we were raised with and inspired by the open and welcoming vibe of our communally-living ancestors. I like to think of our ancestors watching over us in these spaces, smiling down at us as we feast, as we read each other lovingly, knowing that we as queer POC have found community, abundance, connection and joy.

Healing, Reframing, and Reclaiming Your Spiritual Practice

Chapter VI
Queer Witch At Your Service

By Bex Mui

~ One of my favorite offerings as a queer spiritual organizer is to play the role of "floating witch" at queer spiritual and wellness retreats. Think of it like a social worker that you have on hand during a youth gathering. At times, I offer workshops on queering tarot readings, honoring the femme divine of any gender, or decolonizing spirituality. At other times, I might just be there, sending out positive vibes, available for folks who need a moment to recharge or for Reiki or energy clearing. I offer spiritual coaching and consider myself a professional space-holder, with an understanding of a variety of spiritual and religious paths. I also offer energy work including Reiki and chakra clearings, astrology and tarot guidance. In these spaces, I often end up talking to queer and trans people about their strict religious upbringings. I continue to be surprised and delighted by just how many of us in the LGBTQ+ community are holding and navigating some aspect of our spirituality or spiritual and religious upbringings. I especially enjoy connecting and working with queer and trans folks who were raised within strict organized religions. I enjoy reframing deep religious devotion and reflecting on how although Catholicism is no longer my sole container for spirituality, it did carve out grooves in which deep depths of love, desire, and connection can now flow. I consider all of these offerings to be my ministry and the witchy magick that I share with the world.

On some level, I have always known that I was a witch. It took longer for me to understand that this meant I had access to magic, or as it is sometimes called, "magick" to distinguish it from the more common, adopted stuff of spells and imagination as seen everywhere from Disney's fairy godmothers to Urban Outfitters' moon candle collections. Growing up off of Cape Cod meant that I was close enough to Salem for the witch trials to not just be a staple of my English classes through works like *The Crucible*, but also a part of everyday experience, from field trips to family vacations throughout my young, impressionable life.

I don't suppose that everyone on my class field trips or in my family found themselves identifying with the witches from our childhood. In fact, I'm sure that we were taught that this history was distant and foreign, and that it was presented as a cautionary tale. We learned about how these women and girls were outcasted from society, punished for defying the rules of their leaders and their God. But, my baby biracial queer lesbian self was hooked. I saw these women for their power and their magick. I related to them on an instinctual level before I had any words or identities to name it. I honored them for their roles as outcasts, underdogs, and dangerous misfits.

Growing up, I was taught that witches should be feared and the women in the Bible should be silenced, but to believe beyond doubt that I was consuming the actual blood and flesh of Jesus Christ every Sunday. "Cannibalism or bust!" says the Catholic Church. "If you think it's a symbol, then go start your own church, you heretics." — Read: Lutherans It's been a truly shocking curve of my life to see witchy magic become comm-ercialized and mainstreamed, especially among my fellow queers.

Shortly after graduating from college, I moved to New York and found Kristen J. Sollee's *Witches, Sluts, and Feminists* at Bluestockings, a feminist bookstore in the Lower East Side of Manhattan. The book quickly became a Bible for me. Sollee beautifully weaves together what I've always felt and makes connections between these three powerful femme groups that have existed throughout history. She creates a timeline for these archetypes and iterations of witches, femmes who understand sacred sexuality and aren't afraid to make their own magic in the face of patriarchal control.

Today, magic, witches, and powerful women activists and change makers are becoming more and more accepted. In her book *Pleasure Activism*, adrienne maree brown, Patron Saint of Black-Affirming Organizing, wrote a Radical Gratitude Spell, "a spell to cast upon meeting a stranger, comrade, or friend working for social and/or environmental justice and liberation." This book is one of my foundations and something I considered doctrine when I brought it into Queer Church. Reading her words, "You are enough. Your work is enough. You are needed. Your work is sacred. You are here and I am grateful," in the form of a spell, has helped me to bridge the gap between magic and advocacy, belief and action. This has led me to build spiritual support and ritual into my advocacy work. My "self-care" also shifted—from bubble baths to moon rituals, from a glass of wine to a glass of water in which I whispered my manifesting intentions, and set in a window overnight under the full moon. ⸺ Not that I don't still enjoy those baths with a glass of wine, mind you.

In *Missing Witches: Recovering True Histories of Feminist Magic*, Risa Dickens and Amy Torok present a global array of powerful women's stories, rituals, and practices from Harlem to Haiti, in support of our ability to learn from our silenced or hidden ancestors and to "restore magic to its rightful place among powerful forces for social, personal, and political transformation." Their work raised my awareness of magical women beyond white Europeans, and explores the connection between witch hunting and anti-feminist colonization. Unearthing these stories has added to my understanding of witchy history and ancestry. I see this understanding as foundational to my spiritual organizing and integral to building intuition and maintaining faith in my ability to direct my life and make change in the world.

105

Whether you identify as a witch, a wizard, a non-binary magic-maker, or even if you don't have an identity term that feels right, please know that you are a powerful, magical being whose thoughts and words shape your world. Drawing upon our own internal ability to make magick, manifest our dreams and direct our lives is a vital yang that balances the yin of calling in for support in our spiritual practices.

Working with the Moon

Throughout my life, I have experienced the immense power of staying open and saying "yes" over and over again. I began college in New York as a chemistry major and intended to become a pharmacist. I had never been to New York and had no idea what big cities were like. I had never ridden in a cab or on a bus. I had spent my entire life learning among the same 150 people, living in the same house, in the same small town.

Once I arrived and settled into my dorm, the world opened up for me. It was my first experience with a space in which I could begin directing my own life. While in New York, I realized that I wanted to work with children, so I changed my major, somewhat on a whim, to Education and English. Since then, my career has taken me from teaching to LGBTQ+ advocacy in the schools where I taught to national LGBTQ+ advocacy to LGBTQ+ consulting and spiritual organizing. When I walked away from chemistry, I wasn't anticipating all of these turns. And every once in a while, I remember that I almost went to the Massachusetts College of Pharmacy in Boston and think about where my life might have gone had I stayed closer to home, hadn't suffered through the challenge of starting over again and again, hadn't followed and leaned in to what felt right.

I loved working in national LGBTQ+ advocacy. Realizing that it was time to shift away did not come easily to me. It had felt like a dream come true and was more than I had ever expected for myself as a former elementary school teacher. With advocacy work, I was getting paid to do what I had been doing for free in my own time outside of teaching, and was able to create more change and have a greater reach and more impact. Needless to say, it was so damn hard to admit to myself that I was burned out. Work day after work day wore on me like I was in a constant state of crisis management, facing internal, external, interpersonal and systemic struggles. Although it felt important to be a part of the community I was fighting for, it also meant that the work I was doing was hitting me on an internal level. Over time, and through the pause of the pandemic, I realized that I was giving all of my heart, time, and energy to advocacy and had no means to refuel. It was time for a change.

To help make this change happen, I turned to my simple but powerful foundation of working with the moon and the practice of gently guiding my life through ritual and intention. At the start of the new year, working with the dark moon and its powers of release, I wrote a spell for release that I burned in my fireplace. I kept a journal of my thoughts and intentions to remind myself of what I wanted. With the next full moon I asked for the clarity, strength and courage I needed to find a new direction. I kept this practice of building with the energy of the full moon and releasing with each dark moon, journaling at each phase about what I wanted and where I wanted to go next. The moon phases were gentle reminders that created accountability for me. My moon journal reminds me of what I truly want in life and gives me opportunities each month to work towards those goals.

Finding the Moon

There's no doubt in my mind that I wouldn't have changed my career if I hadn't been working with the moon as a spiritual practice. I love that this practice draws on my Chinese heritage of lunar calendars, my witchy beliefs in the moon's pull and power, and my astrological practice of marking time, seasons, and phases. It's also a queer language and more easily accessible to my radical advocacy community than Catholic calendars, and I fully respect that. Whoever we are, whatever our backgrounds are, the moon provides us with a guiding light and fuels us with its energy. It pulls our planet's oceans, makes our tides, and pulls our own water-filled bodies.

It's a disservice to us as beings that we have constructed these concrete habitats that make it difficult or even impossible to see the moon at night. While I was living in New York, I had completely forgotten about the moon. My rhythm was that of the City that Never Sleeps and tied to my work deadlines. I forgot all about nature and for the most part I didn't bother to look up at the sliver of sky that I could see between buildings.

I wasn't following the moon or meditating or checking in with myself. I was working hard, playing hard, and having the time of my life in many ways. I was riding the waves of there being something exciting to do at every moment of every day, and enjoying the ride—in between hangovers and sleepless nights. In 2016, after the presidential election that left so many people in my chosen family heartbroken, I was introduced to the queer astrologer, Chani Nicholas. Chani's horoscopes were my introduction to connecting to the moon and my first experience with lunar astrology. Chani's were also the first horoscopes I read that weren't published in the back of *Cosmo*, and where I learned about rising and moon signs. As a full-time professional social justice advocate and a biracial queer lez trying to make it on my own in a big city that didn't care if I survived, even my joy sometimes felt like a struggle, an effort to find, to maintain or even feel worthy of. Chani's horoscopes spoke to me and helped me to feel seen, held, and guided in a way that I had forgotten I needed. They didn't just write about the stars and the moon, they wrote about the patterns in my inner and outer world. This truly helped me prepare to face the world.

Chani addresses social justice issues and queer people's realities and how the news affects our lives. They didn't comfort me by helping me ignore the world or escape from pain. They helped me face it and acknowledge it and offered insights and recommendations for moving through, even with the world, our government, our country, and power itself being where it was. Over the years, I began to realize that when horoscopes didn't resonate with me, it was because I was rushing rather than reflecting. Tuning in to their horoscopes helped me to stay attuned to myself.

For me, working with the moon and following my calling meant getting out of New York. This realization came when I was in a car headed to Long Island, just outside of the city. Looking out at the trees along the highway, I couldn't stop staring. I got "the feeling—" that nature-appreciation bubble in my heart that I used to get when looking out at the ocean or while standing in the middle of a forest. It was just a patch of trees along the highway, and yet, it was somehow so beautiful to me. I realized then that I had to leave New York. It was time to find somewhere with more space, more green, and more sky.

I made the queer coast-to-coast migration from Brooklyn to the Bay in 2018. I've moved, changed, and shifted in community a few times over the years, but it never seems to get easier to start over. In the Bay, Oakland, Ohlone land to be specific, I found more space for magick to breathe into my life. Nothing pushy, which I would have surely rejected, fiery Aries that I am. I started slow, joining friends for queer hikes and learning how to walk on ground that wasn't a sidewalk. I met astrologers in real life. I started going to moon ceremonies. Nothing too prescribed or forced. Just gatherings of queer witchy friends who wanted to learn together, mark time with the moon's phases, and build intention-setting into our days together.

About six months after moving to the Bay, I was gifted my first tarot-ish deck, Kim Krans' *Animal Spirit Deck*. It has tarot themes but doesn't follow the more commonly used *Smith-Waite Deck*. Knowing very little about tarot as a practice, outside of a random reading in a lesbian bar in NYC years ago, I didn't even know that I was working with a form of a tarot deck in my daily pulls. Then, in 2017, I happened upon an affirmation deck which I promptly brought to my office. I routinely forced—er, strongly encouraged—folks to take a break from their computers, gather around my cubicle, and pull cards. I was always amazed by the ways that the cards put words to feelings and thoughts that were present in a space. Now I'm five tarot decks, two oracle decks, and two affirmation decks in, and still counting. I'll share more about tarot later, but I wanted to mention it here because it was definitely part of my shift at this time when I was—without fully realizing it—opening myself up to magick as a belief system. I was building a practice, sharpening the intuitive tools I needed to make that life shift, leaving my job and taking a chance on myself.

Building Moon Community

Working with the moon to make a change and leave my job was one step. Figuring out what to do next and how to build my spiritual organizing was another. For this, I definitely needed more time and space to sit with myself. When I moved to the Bay, I kept my LGBTQ+ advocacy job in NYC, meaning that I was one of the few folks actually doing remote work prior to the COVID-19 pandemic. This also kept me going back to the NYC office at least once a month for a year and a half. For me, part of the shock of the 2020 "shelter in place" restrictions involved coming to the realization that I actually lived on the West Coast. The pandemic brought up a lot for many of us, and is an experience that will likely live with us for the rest of our lifetimes. In addition to highlighting already -present inequalities and unjust systems in our country and across the world, the pandemic has been an unmistakable reminder that we are fragile animals who for the first time in a long time—in my lifetime—are moving through a universal experience, facing a shared threat that has no care or regard for the borders or boundaries that we've created as humans.

Like so many others, when 2021 hit I was *indignant* that time had passed, wondering where the last eight months of 2020 had gone. I was shocked that time was still there, moving on, while I was feeling so incredibly stuck. It's part of what helped me to realize that I needed a change, and the change I needed was putting into action the spiritual organizing that I'd been building over the last few years. That's why I started House Of Our Queer on Instagram and began the IG Live offering "Queer Church." I missed marking time in community and drew way back to my Catholic roots, when, even if we had nothing else, we always had the Third Sunday in Ordinary Time to keep us on track.

I remember sitting on my girlfriend's couch on January 1st, hovering over the share button and hesitating, wondering if I was truly going to bring Queer Church offerings to my mostly left-leaning, activist, queer and trans friends. Sure, I'd been speaking and writing at the intersection of spirituality and LGBTQ+ culture for years. I'd already written the blog "Coming Out as Queer and Spiritual" years ago. But something about this project felt different. I knew that launching House Of Our Queer would involve approaching this work in a new way, and would hold me accountable to maintaining the rituals and practices I had promised to keep to, and could actually help me to build my queer spiritual community.

Of course I paused.

The thing about rituals, traditions, and even energies as powerful as moon energy, is that there is even more power in doing this work together. There's a reason that churches, synagogues, and mosques exist; it lies in their power as communities. When we engage in ritual with each other, the energy we stir up increases. Humans have an incredible ability to create and shape our worlds with our perspectives and what we believe. Following the moon not only can help us to mark the passing of time, but can help us shift our perspectives from that of powerlessness, victimhood, and defeat to power and strength in the face of life's constant changes. Regularly following the moon plays a central role in maintaining my mental health and inner stability.

By this point, you're probably ready for real, concrete steps. Some of you witches are screaming, "You had me at moon!" Relax, dear reader, I have steps for you. But the most important thing is that you cultivate your own relationship with the moon. There are many ways, and different people and traditions each engage differently. Find ways to follow and work with the moon's phases that work for you.

For me and on Queer Church, we focus on the full moon and new/dark moon. For about two weeks a month, the moon is waxing or growing full, and then for two weeks it is waning, or slowly becoming darker. As the moon grows, I spend time and energy imagining what I want to build, what I want to manifest, and what I would like to have more of in my life. I imagine the full moon bursting with fully charged manifestation power. Every month, I tap into this energy, focusing on what I want to build, where I want to direct my energy, and which areas of my life require my immediate attention. As the dark moon approaches, I use the waning moon to think about what I need to release. What am I doing or holding on to or owning that isn't serving me anymore? What patterns or connections do I need to shift or break? It's a great time to release and to let things go, because directly after the dark moon is a new moon. For many Pagans and witches like me, as soon as the moon begins to grow that crescent of illumination in the night sky, that's the new moon and a signal that the cycle is starting all over again.

What Can You Do?

I. Honor Your Inner Magick

From moon rituals to tarot pulls to spell-casting, all of this work centers around you and your intuition. The "success" of these practices depends on your ability to tap into what you want your life to be, what you want in it, and who you want to connect with. Success also requires trusting that you are worthy of all that you ask for. It's okay to start small, like simply tracking the full moon just to look up at it and remember that you are a sacred and powerful being.

II. Create Your Own Moon Rituals

There are so many ways to work with the moon and stars. I'm not an astrologer, but if you're looking for a professional opinion and want more direct guidance, I recommend checking out Chani Nicholas' work or finding an astrologer whose interpretation of the sky makes sense for you. I truly believe that what's most important is intention and consistency. Try something for a year, and then adjust it if it's not serving you. Try out different types of rituals, and see what feels powerful and offers guidance for you. Connect with friends to share what you're building, what you're releasing, or to join in ritual together.

III. Building With the Moon

There is nothing greater or more powerful than being honest with ourselves about what we truly want. I've spent a lot of time in my life calling in things that I feel that I'm supposed to want, and being dissatisfied once I get them. As a girl, as a Chinese girl, as an immigrant girl, as a femme, I have to field so many messages about what my life should be, who should be in it, and what I need to accomplish to feel worthy of love.

I've called in relationships—just so I didn't feel alone—that I ended up not wanting. I've spent a lot of time and energy and effort perfecting my social skills and extroversion just to realize that I enjoy my own company. Now, when I build with the moon, I do my best to center and ground myself first. I try my best to clear out the expectations of my parents, my girlfriend, and my community or chosen family. The goals that I have for my life are my own, and those around me who truly love me will support me in what I want.

What Can You Do?

◊ Look up when the next full moon will be, and what sign it will be in. Learn indigenous names for this full moon and what they mean. Mark it on your calendar and spend some time in the days leading up to the full moon asking yourself these questions:

> > What do I want to build?
> > Where do I want to lean in and grow?
> > What do I wish I had more of in my life?

◊ You can answer these questions in the form of a journal, a tarot spread, or discussions with friends and chosen family.

◊ It can be helpful to choose one area of your life—career, love and relationships, health, family, etc.—to focus on during the waxing phase leading up to the full moon. In the past, I've asked for direction, clarity, or even just patience with myself. Remember that this is only for the next two weeks, so it's okay to set small goals. You can ask the moon for whatever it is that you're craving, that you want in your core. Manifesting with the full moon is a time to take a moment out of our anxiety-fueled, self-doubting lives and connect to what we truly want in life.

◊ Create a mantra for what you want to build. This can be as simple as

> *I deserve more time for myself.*
> *I am open and ready to receive love.*
> *I want connection.*
> *Please let me be seen and held.*

◊ Fill a cup of water. Place this water in a window that will be most likely to catch the moon's rays. Speak your mantra or manifestation goal into the water, this little receptor for the moon's rays. In the morning, repeat your mantra and drink the cup of water. As you drink, imagine yourself achieving your goal and lean in to the warm, affirming feelings that it brings.

If you're in a windowless room like I was in my early Brooklyn days, just place it wherever you feel the most energy in your space.

IV. Releasing With the Moon

Our consumerist society constantly encourages us to live with a scarcity mindset. It wants us to feel that we are lacking and that we need things in order to be happy, to be complete, to "arrive." Because we are all so powerful, especially as we continue to build ritual and intention into

115

our lives, this can result in us pulling in and grasping for wants that feel like needs, until we are overwhelmed by the results. When I left my full time job in national LGBTQ advocacy to start my own consulting practice and focus on spiritual organizing, I was terrified to not have a steady income or health insurance. Let's face it, having a job as a queer person of color, especially in LGBTQ advocacy, already felt like more than I ever deserved to ask for. Operating in my fear and scarcity mindset, I called in all of the support I could find for work, money, and connections, and spent the first few months of what should have been a well-deserved break and pleasant shift in work-life balance, drowning in abundance. I was overwhelmed by opportunities and it took time for me to refocus and remind myself of why I had made the shift and what I actually wanted to do with my time and energy. While it's important to build, we need to balance building with regular opportunities to let go, to shed, and to release patterns, positions, beliefs, actions, and items that are no longer serving us.

What Can You Do?

◊ Look up when the next dark or new moon will be, and what sign it's in. Read about the indigenous names for this dark or new moon and their meanings. Mark it on your calendar and spend some time in the days leading up to it asking yourself these questions:

> Where is my energy going?

> Is that serving me?
> What am I carrying or holding
  on to that needs to be released?
> What old stories or narratives am
  I telling myself that are harming
  me or keeping me from growth?

◇ You can answer those questions in a journal,
  through a tarot spread, or with friends and chosen family.

◇ Remember that change doesn't happen overnight. If only we could shift our narratives and
  stories, and let go of hurt, pain, and trauma in a
  single moon cycle. But there is power in identifying and naming what we're holding on to, and
  naming what we want to shift or release, regardless of how long it takes to heal.

◇ Destroy it. One simple and powerful ritual for
  letting go of your burdens alongside the dark
  moon is to write them down or represent them
  in some way and to get rid of them, rip them
  up, or burn them. Watching something turn
  to nothing is a reminder of the ways that all
  the things that we are carrying, including the
  narratives that are harming us, can disappear
  with our energy, intention, and support.

V. Stay Open

Like many lessons in this lifetime, I learned this
lesson the hard way. I was once in a relationship
that I was not ready to let go of. I had put a lot of
hopes, dreams, and security into our partnership, our little apartment, and our cat. I can't
tell you how many moons and moon rituals I

spent calling in for patience or security or whatever I thought would help me keep my partner.
I spent so many dark moons asking myself to let
go of jealousy, release ownership, and release
anything that was keeping me from *making this
relationship work*. Ah friends, if only the moon and
our manifestations worked that way. We can direct our lives, we can shift our perspective, and
we can actively move towards things that serve us
and away from things that aren't working. What
we can't do is predict the future and prevent
change from happening, or prevent the pain
and suffering that is part of life.

◊ I'll never forget when I was doing a manifesting ritual with my friend and magical being. We were in her car, under the
full moon, ready to light a candle and call
in our goals, wishes, and desires. We were
ready to receive all that we wanted to come
to us. I was listing away, holding a lighter,
and before I could light the wick, she added, "And for those things we don't yet know
that we need or want." A little space, a little
trust, a little openness in your goal can make
a big difference.

VI. Mark it

Knowing where the moon is and what is coming
up astrologically has shifted my relationship to
work and has altered my otherwise perpetual-
ly-packed social calendar. I don't always spend
the evening of the full or dark moon focused on
ritual, but knowing when it is helps me to shape
what plans I do say yes or no to, and to build in

at least a few moments for self-reflection and ritual. Even if you can't do a ritual on each of these days throughout the year, knowing where the moon is always helps me to extend grace to myself. If the moon is full and I'm applying for something or asking for a raise, I feel a little extra push behind me knowing that the moon is aligned with my actions. Even if that extra push is simply my own confidence, it doesn't hurt!

◊ Research the moon's phases for the coming year. Add these dates to your own queer holiday calendar, with particular focus on the full and new moon of each month.

VII. Keep a Moon Journal

I've been following the moon for years, hopping in and out of moon ceremonies or gatherings by fellow queer witches and astrologers, and keeping track of when the next phases were coming up. When I started to see a real difference, however, is when I began keeping a moon journal. This simple practice has helped me to keep record of what I am building and releasing, where I want to go and what I want to leave behind. While I have to be careful not to use it as a way to feel bad about myself or to induce feelings of failure when repeating goals or wants, keeping track and reflecting each month has made a huge difference for me.

VIII. Follow House Of Our Queer

Since that hesitant post at the beginning of 2021, House Of Our Queer has become a real community. I offer IG live sessions and posts about following the moon and share guidance about how each moon is connected to an astrological sign. I intuit prayer spells for our community around the moon, and offer tarot spreads with specific guiding questions. These are real-time offerings, which help queer and trans folks work with the seasons and what is currently going on in our world. I create moon journals and moon calendars to help us keep track together. Check it out at *HouseOfOurQueer. com* and follow me on Instagram so we can build these practices together!

121

Chapter VII

Queer Spiritual Practices: Astrology and Tarot

By Bex Mui

~ While the name *Queer Church* draws directly from my Catholic roots and rituals, designed for reclamation, its focus each week is largely based on practices and offerings that make use of astrology and tarot. I made that choice intentionally. While the term "queer church" felt spicy, and in this strange way, radical enough for a weekly LGBTQ-centered gathering, I wanted to focus on offerings that make use of spiritual mediums that I see being used more frequently in our community.

Every week, I find a queer-centered reading to consider spiritually. The readings range from

Mary Oliver poems to Buddhist teachings to quotes from Marsha P. Johnson. I want to build my own scripture, with a wider scope and with roots in queer and trans resilience. These readings give way to spiritual questions and reflections for us to hold as we make our way throughout the week. I missed this aspect of church, the teachings, the wonderings, the ways that the homily—the priest's interpretation of the gospel for the week—if done well, took this ancient story and helped us apply it to our everyday lives and experiences.

In Queer Church, these considerations are often shaped by astrology and the moon cycle. I wanted to bring astrology into this weekly offering to help guide some intention into the way that we as a queer community interact with the stars. I see our charts as valuable information and the ever-changing seasons and moons as offering new possibilities. In Queer Church, I offer astrological considerations that give us more questions than answers and that broaden how we see and understand ourselves and our relationships or connections. For example, while there are stereotypes for Leos—and, let's face it, most of the sun signs—there is so much beyond these stereotypes that makes each sign unique and powerful. Leos are represented by the sun, and highlight the ways that we can shine from wherever we are. While the stereotype of Leos "deleting selfies to make room for more selfies" isn't necessarily out of line, it only represents one type of Leo. I offer astrology insights to allow us to consider what the signs and seasons mean for us all, and to expand the way that we work with and understand our charts.

Every week, I close Queer Church with a tarot card pull to guide us into the week ahead. It's a moment to pause while we're together virtually. It's an opportunity to hone in on collective energy. And tarot, if nothing else, is a tool for putting meaning into a moment with words, patterns, and symbols. I bring this practice along with astrology, into Queer Church because I understand both astrology and tarot to be queer

123

spiritual practices, methods that many of us in our community turn to for answers, guidance, and support. Such tools help us have a shared language. And for me, astrology and tarot are religious and spiritual practices, and hold that space for many of us in the LGBTQ community, whether we've thought of it that way or not.

Astrology

It's important to note that I am not a professional astrologer, nor do I have aspirations to become one. Astrology speaks to me through my connection to the moon. Astrological birth charts complement my intuitive understanding of the patterns in my life and the connections we make as humans. Astrology's calendar adds depth to my own queer calendar. Keeping track of when eclipse season begins, and what major transitions are happening are ways that I remind myself and others to be gentle with ourselves, to take breaks, to not rely on technology, and to be extra patient with communication.

Astrology is one tool among many that I use to better understand myself and others. I've looked into my astrological chart, my Chinese astrological signs, ← Yes, there's more than my Myers-Briggs, enneagram, human one sign if you dig deeper design, and more. In Chinese astrology, I was born in the year of the Ox, an earth branch in a metal year. You name it, and I've investigated myself and those around me (with permission). I'm deeply drawn towards self-exploration and better understanding how and why I show up in connection. As a weird child who never really felt that I fit in, I've spent most of my life trying to understand what is expected of me in different situations, and learning how to better navigate social situations. The funny thing is, in each of these systems, my "results" or explanations are eerily similar. In Myers-Briggs, arguably the least spiritual of these tools, I'm an ESTJ, and my official type is called "the executive." I'm not saying that it doesn't fit, but every video I could find to learn more about myself showed some stuffy white man in a suit, some corporate CEO. The world and these systems aren't yet sophisticated enough to take into account the breadth and depth of queer and trans experiences.

That's why I explore them all. My queer spiritual practices are based on and guided by my own intuition, supported by rituals that support all parts of me. I have an ever-growing spiritual toolbox and a curiosity that inspires me to continually learn, grow, and build with myself and others. In astrology, that's explained by my sun sign (Aries), which is the first sign, a fire sign, often characterized by passion and leadership, alongside my rising sign (Capricorn), a grounded "steam-roller" of an earth sign, characterized by approaching goals in a calculated and organized way. The kicker for me is my Sagittarius moon, the wanderlust of fire signs, which fears 125 stagnation, fueling my path professionally and personally head-first into a variety of consecutive passions.

For me, astrology is the system that accords most with my intuition, and that calls to me at this time. I believe that our sun signs—the signs that represent our inner core—are how we show up in the world as children, and that after puberty our rising signs come more into play, as a new way that we show up in the world. Our moon signs, representing our moods and emotions, are always present and guiding our inner worlds. I used to use sun signs to create my table seating arrangements when I was an elementary school teacher. It was helpful to know which young ones were water signs, which little fires. I wouldn't want to put too many Pisces at a table, unless they got along and were happy to be guided by a gentle Virgo or a reasonable Capricorn. When I taught second grade in Beijing, China, I received my student roster with their birth order, with the cultural understanding that first born children had significantly different traits and considerations than middle or youngest siblings.

I am a fan of having more tools. I like that we have birth charts, far beyond our sun, moon, and rising signs, that help to explain how we move through this world, what drives us, and how we seek connection. In addition, the stars and the planets are always moving, so these charts and meanings aren't stagnant. They move and flow and are ever-changing. Our lifetimes are flowing through an ever-evolving and cyclical opportunity to shift and grow.

I only use astrology in an expansive way. I speak adamantly against sun-sign stereotyping in the queer community and beyond. There are no bad signs. There are no bad matches. And if there were, I don't believe our charts are designed to tell us. I recently had someone ask me to look at their chart, saying, "I know it says I'm a lone wolf, but I don't want that to be true." Our charts don't tell us what we are or aren't. They don't label or brand us, and we shouldn't cause harm to ourselves or others by using these incredibly enigmatic tools to put people in boxes. Our charts won't say we're a "lone wolf," but they may indicate that we value independence over partnership, that we are cautious with our hearts and that we need security to fully show up for others, or that we make our best decisions after intuitive alone time.

— Yes, even you, Geminis.

126

As with partnerships or long-term connections, I don't believe the stars are invested in telling us who to date. Especially when it comes to sun sign compatibility, we can Google ourselves into a panic that no one needs to add to modern dating. I'll take a moment to call out the Costar app for this—yes you, Costar, with your smile, meh, and frown symbols telling people how their chart compatibility ranks. There are some great functions for this app, especially their personal charts and connection to the houses, but compatibility isn't one of them. When I look at astrology charts and see so-called "compatibility," what I actually see is examples of how people will likely flow easily or are similar to another person, or ways that they approach areas from a different way and will need more understanding and communication, providing opportunity for growth. For example, the way that I approach challenges, partnerships, communication, etc., may be similar to you. But that doesn't mean that matching with someone and getting all "smiles" is the goal. I once compared charts with a coworker and we were shocked to find that our charts were basically identical. We were friendly and collaborative as coworkers, but certainly were not besties like this "jackpot" of a reading might suggest. What it meant was that we are very similar. We play similar roles to the people in our respective lives, creating connection and partnership and community in similar ways. What our results don't mean is that the two of us are fated to be together.

As for those "meh" and sad faces, those challenging aspects that compatibility readings love to scare folks with? Bring them on! Think of those as areas where you approach things from opposite angles, where you might push each other to grow, and where you might remind yourselves to have extra patience, clear boundaries, or openness to compromise so as to avoid having the same arguments over and over again.

Looking at your chart on your own or in partnerships (professional, intentional, emotional, intimate, sexual, or any combination) can support reflection and communication. It's a tool to help you dig deeper, notice patterns, and direct your life, not a life sentence or a lottery ticket. I'd love to give a deeper example, but my girlfriend has forbidden me from looking at her chart in depth, and I respect boundaries. But what I can say is that she's a Capricorn, a grounded earth sign, which is also my rising sign, or how I show up with others. She's also a Scorpio moon and rising. — I know, right? Scorpios are heart-led water signs represented by an animal that can sting you to death. She is not subtle. To people with charts run by or full of water, especially the flowy water of Cancer or Pisces, she might show up as fiery or even guarded. Scorpios can get a bad rap for being manipulative, but in truth, they know what they want, they know how to get it, and they aren't interested in making a big fuss or show of it. My chart is mostly fire, some earth and the only — Bless you, water in my chart is two Scorpio placements. grounding My girl may be intense, but her intensity reads in my chart. like water and heart to me.

Cap placements

I also read astrology charts with a Chinese lens for balance. I rely heavily on the balance—or imbalance—between the elements of water, earth, air, and fire, and what it means for us and those that we are in relationships with. I use this balance when it comes to tarot as well, since each suit represents an element. This approach is a valuable method that allows me to read charts and tarot without negative or threatening interpretations. While I still get a kick out of Scorpio memes and the Aries videos my friends send me practically daily, I insist that we don't have to blame everything on Mercury being in retrograde, or exclusively shape our relationships on sun-sign compatibility. Astrology is a practice that offers us information about what comes naturally to us, when we will approach situations in a similar or different way than another person, and insights into what rules our communication, our sense of self, and who and how we love.

What Can You Do?

I. Find Your Birth Chart

There are a lot of free apps you can use to find your birth chart, including Costar, The Pattern, Time Passages, and The Chani App. If nothing else, knowing your birth chart, especially your

sun, moon, and rising signs, can help you answer questions that will inevitably come up on
first dates and at queer parties.

II. Guide Your Own Exploration

Don't just read one version of your chart. Study
your chart using a few different apps, online,
and even consider checking out some of the
other personality and self-discovery options I
mentioned earlier, like Chinese astrology, Human Design, Enneagram, and Myers-Briggs.
Hold everything you read with some openness.
Raise questions to reflect on based on what you
read, thinking broadly about your reaction style,
how you show up in spaces, and what patterns
you may be repeating in connecting to others
and yourself.

129

III. Look Into Your Houses

While our signs and planets all have charged
meanings, houses are just areas or placements
in the sky where our chart exists. I think of
houses as our own personal light shows in the
sky. The sky is divided into 12 houses, and our
chart overlays that, either lighting up in houses—or not. Each house has a different guiding
focus, and I believe that digging into them is
one tool for helping us to better identify our
purpose in this lifetime. Most of my friends
who are backpackers, folks who find comfort
in bringing all of their belongings in a sack
on their backs, don't have much, if anything,
in the 2nd house, which is ruled by the mantra "I have" and is connected to valuing money,
property, and possessions. That doesn't mean

that having a stacked 2nd house makes you vain or materialistic. Houses simply offer clues regarding the greater meaning behind our signs and ruling planets.

IV. Use Astrology to Expand, Not Stereotype

Have I been personally burned by a Gemini? Yes. Do I subscribe to @notallgeminis? Yes. Am I sent Aries memes on the regular in ways that read me to absolute filth? 100% yes, all the time. Like many stereotypes, astrology stereotypes play on some form of truth, and we can find connection, humor, and meaning in them. And like all stereotypes, they can be harmful if we take them too seriously, for ourselves or for others. Nothing about your life is finished or set in stone while you are still living it.

Man, my friends are jerks sometimes.

Tarot

I recently had an intuitive tarot reader and dear friend, Jessica Higgins @Teachntarot, join Queer Church to talk about and share the many decks that have found their ways into our lives, and the slightly different purposes they serve. When I asked her how she started using tarot as a practice, she said that she, like many folks who are drawn to tarot cards, had experience with them in a past life and sought them out in this life as a tool for guidance, and to awaken the intuition for directing her life.

I mentioned earlier how the cards found me, first affirmation cards and later *The Wild Unknown Animal Spirit Deck* by Kim Krans. The beautiful imagery on that deck shows different animals from the earth, air, water, and desert (fire) and helped me to better understand the balance of the elements in traditional tarot. In my experience, each animal has represented a message that I needed to hear, whether it was the water's frog, representing clearing and cleansing and encouraging release and forgiveness, or the bat (similar to the death card in traditional tarot) that reminded me of the beauty of waiting in the darkness for the sun to rise, confident in my ability to adapt, adjust, and welcome a new day, or a new change on the horizon.

Each reading ended with the card's meaning when in balance and out of balance, alongside ways to create balance. This gentle reading is something that I bring to all of my tarot readings. Sure, the devil can be a scary card to pull—especially for us Christian-rooted folks—but, in essence it simply signifies that we may be leaning too far into our indulgences, and serves as a reminder to reset and consider moderation in our actions to restore balance. When I do a tarot reading, I am reminded that, however sharp the message, however hard a pill it is to swallow, there is always a way to bring the situation back into balance.

131

I've been pulling cards daily for years, and I intuit tarot spreads for moon cycles, manifesting, and finding ways to let go. I love how a tarot spread can help me to center myself. It helps me to become rooted and to ask the questions that are on my mind. It gives me a chance to interpret what I pull, to put words to some of the thoughts, feelings, or patterns in my life, and to build in reflection and accountability as time passes. Whether or not you believe in the energy or magick of the cards themselves, these practices can help when you feel stuck, confused, and hurt.

The thing is, the cards don't lie. They're sharp and quick and scarily accurate if you build a practice of asking open questions. They help me stay connected to the actual pace of change, even when it hurts. I may feel like I'm over a breakup or a lost job opportunity. I'll have Lizzo's "Good as Hell" on repeat and hop out of bed, feeling optimistic, and there it is again, the Three of Swords with its undeniable, stabbed and broken heart. I used to resent these patterns, these reminders of my own inner truth. Over time, however, I use them to be patient with myself and to better attune myself to the reality that making peace takes time, that evolving is cyclical, and that it is okay to still be holding hurt or pain, or to take time to process heavy feelings. After years of pulling, it has started to feel comforting when the cards "read" me—even drag me—because there is comfort in feeling seen when I'm in pain.

Lately, I've been pulling the Nine of Swords on repeat. Swords are particularly sharp ⟵ no pun intended with their meanings and their imagery. The Nine of Swords usually depicts some version of swords hanging horizontally on a wall above a figure who is distressed and sitting up in bed. Pleasant, right?

The thing is, as intense as this card can be, its message is a warning and an offering for our consideration. It lets us know that our negative thoughts and worries are getting the best of us, and warns us of the self-fulfilling prophecy that can come as a result. It also offers us a way to find balance, to get out of this cycle. It does so by reminding us of the power of our thoughts to direct our actions, and therefore our lives. It encourages us to not just dismiss our negative thoughts, or internalize them, but to actively think positively for a time, to lean on optimism. My trauma response is to be on high alert for any and all signs that something is wrong, that something needs my attention, something that I can change. This card, as scary as it looks, is actually a strong suggestion that I chill the fuck out, calm my mind, and let life unfold as it will. It's a reminder I've needed a lot lately, but change takes time.

Tarot Roots

There is no general consensus about the original creation of tarot cards, but I'm in the camp of believers who trace the roots back to ancient Egypt, with spiritual foundations near the Great Pyramid of Giza, the same place where three major religions surviving today—Judaism, Islam, and Christianity—were born. From these roots, this magick was developed through a card game developed by Bahri Mamluks, who were mainly natives of southern Russia. My limited understanding follows the cards from Turkey to Western Europe in the 14th century, likely through Venice. The word "tarot" is believed to come from the river Taro in Northern Italy, where the first known tarot deck was reported in 1442. In the late 1700s, the very first guide to tarot reading was published by Jean-Baptise Alliette and since then the cards have become used for more spiritual purposes as opposed to being used like a typical card game.

133

The "Waite-Smith" deck, often referred to as the "Rider Waite"or "Rider-Waite-Smith" deck, published in 1909, is the most well-known and "traditional" tarot deck used today. It was drawn by Pamela Colman Smith, nicknamed Pixie, who was a British artist, writer, and feminist activist. She is often erased from this narrative, with more focus placed on the author, mystic Arthur Edward Waite, and the publishing company, The Rider Company. The symbolism created in this deck provides the foundation for modern tarot interpretations.

In her book, *Modern Tarot: Connecting with your Higher Self Through the Wisdom of the Cards*, **Michelle Tea** discusses the symbolism in Smith's imagery, the meaning for each of the 78 cards, and shares a spell or ritual for working with each message. Tea writes in her introduction, "Tarot offers moments of deep connection during a time when connection is ubiquitous but rarely delves beneath the surface... Tarot reminds us of the circular nature of things, how emotions rise up but fade away, how trouble comes but is replaced by luck, which is once again unseated by hardship. Ideally, such a study in the relative impermanence of it all helps us loosen our grip on whatever we're painfully trying to stave off or pull towards us."

The sentiment that Michelle Tea is hitting on here, that the practice of tarot can bring to our lives, is fundamentally a Buddhist principle of the beauty in letting go. Pema Chödrön, beloved queer Buddhist teacher and author, encourages us to accept the cycles of life, to welcome change, and to find joy in letting go. She tells us, "The essence of generosity is letting go. Pain is always a sign that we are holding on to something—usually ourselves." I'd add, usually old, outdated, and limiting versions of ourselves that are no longer serving us. In tarot, this is represented by the Wheel of Fortune, my birth card, which reminds us that change is constant and that the wheels of our lives are always turning. Whether we are in joy or sorrow, the tides will turn. Take time to pause and appreciate when we experience joy, and hold on to hope when experiencing sorrow. All tarot card pulls can be gentle (or strong) reminders to reframe, let go, shift, or make a change.

I'm not surprised by the prevalence and resurgence of tarot in mainstream culture. As Michelle Tea puts it, "Our future-focused, technology-obsessed world seems to be hurtling down a bad path. People are turning to ancestral practices for a sense of enduring longevity, and comfort ... To source a different kind of power in hopes of making changes both personal and political." I believe that many queer and trans people are here in this lifetime to break patterns of ancestral trauma. It makes sense that we are seeking tools like astrology and tarot, making activist magic, and challenging institutional systems of oppression while honing our own spiritual growth.

We need spiritual systems that center
our own intuitions, and need spiritual
language, ritual, community and connection
that isn't rooted in patriarchal, cis and
heterocentric oppression and leadership.

I stand for astrology and tarot as queer spiritual practices, and also enourage those who practice to know their roots, and to engage in practices with intention. Pulling cards is an active meditative practice, something that coupled with keeping a tarot journal to record daily pulls and moon ritual spreads, has, for me, become a solid foundation for self-guided intuition-building and pursuing life goals. Tarot combines the practice of connecting to higher powers to ask for support with being reminded of my own strength, power, and ability to make change in my life, world, and community.

135

What Can You Do?

I. Don't Pull for the Future

Tarot works best as a practice of supplying words, patterns, and meanings to answer questions you currently have on your mind. While it can offer some future glimpses or "if this continues then..." insights, tarot is not a fortune-teller or a Magic 8-Ball. Especially while still early on in developing a practice, the more open-ended you are with questions, and the more thought you put into the multiple meanings the cards can offer, the more you can get out of reading as a form of self-reflection.

II. Choose Your Decks

One deck that helped me to see myself in tarot as a queer, biracial, social justice activist was the Next World Tarot deck by Christy C. Road. This incredible, intuitive deck features inspiring and unquestionably evocative illustrations on each card. The figures shown are inspired by real queer, trans, Black, indigenous and people of color activists, mostly based in Brooklyn, NY. Her booklet of interpretations emphasizes messages for taking action, inspiring collective change, and developing resilience in a systematically unjust world. This deck is essentially my Chani-interpretation-of-the-stars, but for tarot instead of astrology. There are other differences from traditional decks, such as the "suspension" card being used in place of the typical "hanged man," as used in the Smith-Waite deck. Although this card is more about a moment of pause, a reminder that we can release ourselves from the trap of a moment, whether with change or even a perspective shift, the traditional image of a person hanging from a noose can be triggering for some folks. In Road's deck, this card is renamed "suspension" and features a person in an upside-down position against a pink sky, hanging on to a silver horseshoe by the back of one knee. The hanged man imagery is also addressed in Lisa Sterle's Modern Witch Tarot deck, a deck that echoes some of the imagery created by Smith, while replacing the figures with mostly women of color, and adding in modern twists like laptops, cellphones, and great outfits. Sterle includes the rope featured in the original imagery, but highlights a girl in fishnets hanging upside-down, chillin, with the rope snug around her ankle.

<u>Note</u>

If we must fuel capitalism through this practice, let's do so with intention. If you are interested in a deck, find out who is making it, and if they identify with the culture or twist that they've created. Track where the money is going. Do your research to see if your purchase can be made directly from the producer or from a small local magick shop near you. If you're buying a deck that's part of a culture you're not a part of, consider what your connection is, and how you can spend time, money, and resources giving back to that community outside of the deck purchase.

III. Consider the Imagery

137

The images on the cards are a significant part of the practice of reading. Some artists use more realistic imagery, whereas others are more artistic and interpretive. When considering which deck (or next deck) is for you, you might also think about if you want more "traditional" Smith-Waite type imagery, or less traditional art. One asset to using an iteration of the Smith-Waite deck is that it may help you to learn the meanings faster. I have a beautiful Antique Anatomy deck by Claire Goodchild, whose scientific drawings and twists like "elixirs" for cups speak to me. I got this deck at the start of the pandemic in early 2020, and the juxtaposition of bones, skeleton parts, and bright, blooming flowers gave my readings the right tone. However, without the classic imagery, people, and symbols featured on the Smith-Waite cards, it's harder to remember and intuit the meanings of the pulls.

IV. Pull With Intention

I'll never forget the shock and disgust I felt when I was at a Halloween costume store and noticed that they were selling Halloween-store-branded "tarot decks." Decks like these are a symbol of capitalism at its finest, removing the magick and ritual and history from this practice. Regardless of whether you choose a deeply meaningful ancestral deck or a kitschy cat people deck, it's important to pull cards with intention. Remember, you get what you give in terms of ritual and practice. Before you pull, it's helpful to calm and ground yourself, even doing a little meditation to clear your mind. Hold the cards in your hands and state your intention for the pull. Ask a question, whether it's something specific you're looking for guidance around, or something general like, "What do I need to hear?" which is the question I use for my daily pulls. Shuffle the cards while you meditate on that question or focal point. When you're ready, stop and pull the top card.

V. Intuit Your Own Meaning

One time, after a breakup from a relationship in which I had been living with my partner, I pulled the Five of Pentacles. While pentacles are the earth suit and many cards mean positive fortunes and grounding, the

Five of Pentacles isn't one of them. The card centers around financial loss, hard times, and feelings of isolation and scarcity. I was pulling from the Next World Tarot deck, where this is represented by gentrification. The card depicts a small, hopeless girl looking out of a window that will no longer be her neighborhood, scattered boxes in the foreground. I thought of the boxes I'd soon be using to pack up my own belongings, and the ways the boxes represented the dismantling of the life I thought I'd have with this partner, the home I thought I'd stay in. The traditional Smith-Waite image for the Five of Pentacles is of people being turned away from a church, asking the question, "Where do you turn to when your safety isn't safe anymore?" As someone who has been turned away from my original church, and has attempted to create belief systems and safety out of romantic relationships that didn't last, this meaning added a lot to the pull. It wasn't just about the boxes, the view, the change, the hopelessness. It was the feeling that what I'd hoped was safe wasn't safe anymore. I needed more than a new window to look out of. I needed a whole new definition of safety, security, and grounding.

◊ When you pull a card or spread, take some time to look at the images and illustrations first. If there's a figure, notice their facial expressions and body language. Notice the setting and any symbols that you see. Think about how you feel when looking at the card or cards. Then go ahead and look it up. Each deck will come with their own interpretation of the meaning for each card. One of the benefits of having multiple decks is being able to read a few interpretations for each card. Build your own intuition by reading from multiple sources, including free online resources such as Biddy Tarot, and journal about the meaning as you interpret it. If you could summarize the card as an answer to the question that you asked, what would the advice be? What shift in perspective or overall message are you left with? Remember that the purpose of tarot isn't to tell the future, or to drag you, it's mostly to help wake you up and make yourself accountable to the messages you likely already know and the actions you probably know you need to take.

VI. Take Care of Your Decks

I believe in respecting rituals and magical tools. If you're going to be building a practice with the cards and delving into the ritual of tarot, it is helpful to treat your cards with care. Some witches recommend keeping cleansing crystals with your decks. For example, selenite can be used to clear the energy you stir up by pulls and spreads, while amethyst is used for charging up or strengthening energy, spiritual development, and visioning. Overall, just don't use your deck as a doorstop or shove it in the back of your closet and assume that you'll get the same results out of the daily pulls or spreads you create to seek answers. Your body, mind, and energy know when you're taking something seriously, and that is reflected in the cards.

VII. Start With a Daily Pull

I've mentioned this before, but I feel that it is important to devote time to it here. Doing a daily pull is a great way to dip your toe in the pool of this practice. It can be helpful to do this at the same time each day, whether it's the first thing you do to start and frame your day, just before bed, or when you transition from work to play! Recording pulls can help you to notice themes and trends and to better recall the meanings. I tend to pull the same cards over and over again at certain points in my life. My friends and I usually text each other when we're getting a string of swords, which tend to be harsher both in imagery and message, or if a major card is haunting us.

I get it, Wheel of Fortune! I'm working on it!

141

VIII. Queer it up!

While tarot is, like astrology, a relatively popular practice for queer and trans folks, the decks themeslves and many of the tarot books I've turned to aren't written by or for us. That means I've had to do a lot of translating to read the cards, their meanings, read: labor and what they mean for my queer, gender-expansive, non-monogamous life, and the lives of those I'm in community with. For example, in pulls I will use "connection" instead of "relationship" to be inclusive of the multitude of meaningful human connections, whether asexual, aromantic, intentional, energetic, sexual, romantic, and so on. Decks created by LGBTQ people and especially QTBIPOC folks can help us feel seen. However, you might still have to do some work to interpret a deck's meanings to fit yourself and your own relationships. I like to think of the cards as having masc and femme leanings, but not as being strictly related to men and women. Regardless of how we identify, we all embody different elements of femme and masc energy, expression, and behaviors. Find the interpretations and meanings that fit your life, and the decks (and tarot readers, for that matter) that help you do the least amount of labor.

Chapter VIII Reclaiming Holidays

By Bex Mui

~ One of my core spiritual and mental health practices involves reclaiming and re-imagining holidays for myself. This subject is a touchy one, and it's a practice that I didn't come to easily. Nothing puts a damper on the holiday spirit more than learning about the hidden racist histories of many of our country's national holidays and the way that they were curated as a parade of the "accomplishments" of white cis hetero men throughout history, at the continued erasure of and discrimination against others. I invite you to feel any kind of anger and frustration about this, and I deeply understand feeling disappointment in our country and its systems, including our government. My advice here isn't, "I'm a sometimes white-passing person who grew up near Plymouth where the Puritans first landed so we might as well ignore what we know about history and make holiday cookies."

That being said, many of the folks in my community and in left-leaning circles spend their personal and often professional lives fighting against unjust systems and working to make change. We are well aware and doing what we can both inside and outside of these systems to make change. But what we aren't doing is recharging. As in any community, we deserve to take a break, to pause, and to celebrate.

The fact is, over the course of a year, holidays come up many times. At their essence, holidays are opportunities to mark the passing of time, to celebrate in community, and to build in a practice or routine that sparks joy. When we reject holidays, we inadvertently stack our annual schedule with more time for anger, frustration, and a feeling of dread. This impacts our nervous systems, which as queer and trans people are already strained, likely intensified by other systemic inequalities. It is already difficult to live and thrive in this world that was not built for us. We hold tension in our bodies when we hold our breaths until these holidays pass.

145

We don't need the fear and anger that holidays can bring up in our lives.

But what if we found the roots of these holidays, and reimagined them for ourselves?

What if the New Year was a way to reflect on the year behind us and manifest for the year ahead? Imagine Valentine's Day as a day of radical self-love or loving your community. Honoring love in its abundance, beyond the two-person, romantic narrative. Even the Fourth of July has roots in the concept of freedom and independence, which is a privilege.

I can't make decisions for you about what will work for you and your community. The deep pain of the roots of some of our holidays, like Thanksgiving and Columbus Day, can feel too problematic to reclaim. And yet, these days remain there, reminding us every year of their existence. On these difficult holidays, I use Queer Church as a platform for sharing poems, quotes, and hidden histories of queer indigenous and two-spirit people. I donate and encourage others to donate to local indigenous activist efforts. And I create my own rituals and traditions involving food, gifts, and joy that help me look forward to these moments each year. I often spend such holidays with my chosen family and host anyone in need of a place to be. And I research new ways to be of service to impacted communities, raising awareness and sending donations to local or national organizations. You'll have to find the balance that works for you, for your heart and your mind.

> What I do know is that we in the queer community can be quick to reject. We reject and we push away, but we aren't sure what to put in place of what we reject, which can leave us feeling empty.

If you've had this experience, or if it resonates with you at all, I hope you'll consider taking some steps towards reclaiming.

And I know what you're thinking. This is all fine and good for St. Patty's Day, but what about Christmas and the holiday season? I'll admit it. I adore that time of year. For me, the holiday season starts the day after Thanksgiving. Of course, celebrating Christmas growing up helped me to reshape and reclaim my holiday traditions as an adult. I have a lot of privileges, including having been raised celebrating Christmas, that make the holiday season easier for me to reimagine and redesign. Trust me that I do also understand the deep pain that can come at this time of year, and that it isn't always easy. If you're overwhelmed and simply want to mentally block out the last few months of each year, please, take care of yourself and meet your needs. Reframing doesn't happen overnight. *Please be kind to yourself.*

The following suggestions are drawn from ways that I've reframed aspects of the holiday season. I offer them as tools to help you not merely survive the winter holidays but to reclaim them for yourself.

What Can You Do?

I. Find Something To Look Forward To

Like it or not, the end of the Western calendar year is a time that differs from the rest of the year. Whether celebrating Kwanzaa, Hanukkah, the birth of Jesus, or a more secular Christmas or holiday time, many people are buzzing around, looking forward to the holidays or counting down to something.

Finding your own celebration to look forward to can actually retrain our nervous systems which many of us have learned to tense up, leading to fear and anxiety as the annual "dreaded season" approaches. Proactively creating my own holiday at this time of year, a reimagined version of a holiday that I have roots in, has reminded me that institutions don't control this time of year—or me.

Offering
Find something that feels meaningful to you, and celebrate it every year during the holiday season. Whether that's a reclaimed version of one of these holidays, the winter solstice, a friend-anniversary, or just the closing of the calendar year and the chance to begin anew, find something to look forward to. Part of the joy of this time of year simply involves counting down and

building anticipation. Having your own holiday or celebration around this time can help to ease the feeling of disconnect that can arise during this season.

II. Make Your Own Ritual

Growing up Catholic taught me that there is comfort in ritual. Doing something each year with intention builds our memories of our lives and can create comfort in a world full of uncertainty and things we can't control. Discovering what you want to do around this time, some repeated action that brings you joy, can help you look forward to this time of year, no matter what or who is around.

Offering

Regardless of what you choose to celebrate at this time, you can design what it looks like. Whether that means an involved ritual with intention done with others or a simple action like watching a movie, eating a certain type of food, or visiting a certain park or body of water, find the ritual that feels right to you to close out your year.

III. Build Your Own Holiday Community

I'm one of the lucky ones because I have a close and growing relationship with my biological family. It wasn't easy after coming out, but with space, understanding, and lots of conversations, I'm amazed at the relationships we've built since. That being said, we don't celebrate holidays together. Since college, we've celebrated before or after the actual days, when we don't have to participate in the holiday travel rush or pay unreasonable prices for plane tickets. This has also freed me up to spend holidays with so many different loved ones and chosen family over the years. It's been surprising to me to find out how many people, for so many reasons, don't go "home" for the holidays. For me, shifting my thinking from feeling left out or isolated because I didn't go home to embracing the opportunity to meet and connect with new people each year has made such a huge difference. It has also given me a chance to get to know people I might have otherwise missed.

149

Offering

Start telling folks that you will be around for the holidays or asking what people will be doing. Reach out to people you miss but haven't talked to in a while and see if they want to connect. If you've decided on a ritual or something you want to celebrate, let people know and see if they're interested in joining. Or choose to spend the time solo, giving yourself the gift of silent intentional time to just be with yourself.

IV. Define Presents for Yourself

One thing that has helped me maintain my holiday joy is that I stopped exchanging presents with my bio family after graduating from high school. One of the stresses that can ruin the holiday season is an exchange that glorifies capitalist success or the idea that the value you place on a person or a relationship is related to your ability to guess, purchase, and present the ideal material object that a person wants to own. Personally, when gifts are expected, I'm a terrible gift-giver. I like to give gifts as they feel right throughout the year, not on demand.

Offering

Have a check-in with folks who you exchange gifts with or want to celebrate with. Consider other options for showing that you care about each other at this time of year. You can exchange recipes, poems, songs, or books. My sister and I exchange a new recipe each year, which gives us the opportunity to share about the cooking we've done and have enjoyed over the year. I'm a big fan of experiences as gifts, from a museum day, to a theme park trip, to a longer get-away. Memories and adventures last longer and can have greater impact than objects that fit under a tree. My ex and I used to wrap things up from our house to give to each other every Christmas. She'd gift me a shirt of mine that she liked seeing me in, a yoga mat I owned but hadn't brought out in a while, or a book that I'd bought for myself but had never read. Many of us already live in abundance, and can use this as a time to re-appreciate what we already have. Finally, consider gifts that cost nothing, like a three-hour block of uninterrupted time to paint, a game night, a long walk, or a sleep-in morning.

V. Spread Some Cheer

The collective energy of our country and many places around the world is palpable during the holiday season. Some of our isolation as queers can be due to the fact that we don't tap into that or even reject the feeling because of its Christian origin. Redefining cheer, positive vibes, and even decorating can be a helpful lift at this time. If you're not into Christmas decorations, cut snowflake-like designs from rainbow paper or magazines. Hang up pictures of queer icons or loved ones that you want to keep in your mind at this time. Put up silly pictures or paper chains with jokes on them. Decorations can serve to signify change, brighten our lives, and remind us that this season is a different time and that we deserve to participate in that joy.

151

Offering

Get to the root. At its essence, this can be a time to spread good vibes, smile more, and extend gratitude toward neighbors, friends, and even strangers. Donate more, write affirmation cards or texts, uplift and fund QTBIPOC artists, authors, and activists, or spread cheer or joy in ways that feel meaningful to you.

What Now?

> Print out a calendar or list of holidays. Add in holidays that are a part of your cultural or religious background. For me, this includes Lunar New Year, Qingming—a Chinese holiday for attending to family graves and ancestors—and Lent, which I

reclaimed this year to build in balance and appreciation for treats, time, and experiences in my life that I was taking for granted. For those of you who don't know, during Lent, folks who celebrate often choose to fast from excess for 40 days until Easter.

> Brainstorm new names, perspectives, or rituals to incorporate into these holidays.

> Add in LGBTQ+ holidays. I treat Pride and Folsom as seriously as I treat any other holiday. I don't need to wait for the US government to give me the day off to build ritual and prioritize time with my community each year. I use my sick time. Have a straight wedding or bachelorette party scheduled during that time? Say no. It's a holiday.

> Make your own holidays. Love your birthday? Add it in. Love summer? Add in a solstice celebration and plan an annual picnic in the sun. Value friendship? Have a chosen family reunion every spring. Write it in and engage in some of the rituals you do together to make it special.

> Add a Just You holiday. Why not? Find a day of the year when you can take yourself on a solo trip or go to the movies alone. If there is a national holiday that you don't resonate with, rewrite it as a self-date day and give yourself one day each year where you rest on the advocacy you're prioritizing at other times.

> Celebrate holidays with your community. Whether they're your community for now or for the long haul, celebrating with people can add an extra layer of joy and energy to any reclaimed holiday. Making

and reclaiming in community can help you to re-imagine these days of the year and to look forward to them together.

Chapter IX

Growth Isn't Linear

~ There are ways that this book flowed out of me, and I was often surprised by the words, ideas, and themes that appeared on its pages. In true superstitious form, I've been hesitant to talk about the book with people, unsure of when it would start to feel "real." As I sit down to write this attempted summary of my winding, weaving, path, it also occurs to me that I've been writing this book for my entire life. An avid journal keeper since I was young, and one of the only people I know who can actually maintain those trendy 5-year One Line A Day journals, I've always been reflecting on this lifetime as I'm living it, keeping record of it for myself throughout the years.

That practice partially came out of necessity. It's been complicated to discover myself in this hetero, binary, white-normative world. One of the advantages of being someone whose identities aren't modeled for you is having the freedom and space to figure out who you are over time. I've still never seen a freckled, half-Chinese/Malaysian, half-Polish, queer, lesbian with my brand of hard switchy femme. I've never had a good answer for, "Which actor would play you in the movie of your life?"

Even in the queer spiritual world, I haven't yet found my resting place. In my collective of LGBTQ+ ministers, I'm the queer witch who talks about the moon on Instagram. In my moon ceremonies, I'm the Jesus-advocate who's marking when it's time for reclaimed Lent and bringing the holiday cheer. In the sexual health advocacy community, I'm the spiritual organizer who maintains religious roots while eschewing purity culture, making those wild connections between Catholic devotion and kink culture.

My desk is decorated with a St. Lucy pen-dant, ever-rotating crystals, a series of octopus charms and pendants, and a "Hex the Patriarchy" pin. My desktop background is always some image of the ocean, my sacred calm place. I sit

> Patron Saint of Eyesight who helps me as a visually-impaired person

155

between my ancestor altar and a bookcase that contains my feng shui fish tank, my overflowing box of tarot cards, my femme shrine, my moon ritual and saint candles, and a rib bone that I decorated with the phrase "Queer Joy." I bring all of this to my spiritual practice, and derive energy from each of these items and practices in my current spiritual phase.

This may be the book's closing, but I'm not here to say that I've arrived. I am appreciative of all of the stages of my spiritual journey and its wanderings as I discover myself. I believe fully that our work in this lifetime is primarily about getting to better know and love ourselves and to build our inner intuition to do less harm to ourselves and others. Connecting to our intuition and spiritual core can be incredibly support-ive when growing connections and relationships. Connec-tions and community, whether intimate, emotional, intellectual, physical, sexual, asexual, aromantic, polyamorous, monogamous(-ish), are all central to our experience in this life. Teasing this out can all be done in a spiritual lens.

As a queer person, I'm brought back to spiritual work over and over again. No matter how separate the world may try to make us feel from religion, faith, or spirituality, I know deeply that this work is for us, and that we add great depth to spiritual experience. Queer and trans people, especially those of us with multiple marginalized identities, more layers to uncover outside of whatever society has currently deemed the norm, have extra layers of this work, extra internal digging to do, and much more noise to cancel out along the way. We often aren't meant to stay in the places we are from, and can't always learn these lessons from the people who raise us. I believe that many queer and trans people, especially those of us who are BIPOC and first gen, are here to break some of our families' ancestral and generational trauma patterns; we arrived to forge a fresh start and expansive continuation of our family lineage.

Our lives and spiritual work may not be light. It's not easy to be too big, too complete, too spacious, too nuanced, too uninhibited to be defined (or confined) by the labels, lifestyles, and expectations that seem to fit just fine for our bio families and other people around us. There can be some pain in knowing that you can't live the life that seems to work so well for your loved ones. There are times that I've looked at people with lives that I wasn't fated to live who seem happy and content and clear about the norms that they've taken on or were born into. And in those times I've felt a certain jealousy, or a desire to be them.

And yet, I am ever-grateful for my life, my journey, and the spiritual lessons I continue to learn. I hope that sharing some threads of my story and some offerings along the way has been helpful to you, dear reader. Please take what resonates with you, and leave the rest for another person or perhaps another time. This is not a how-to manual for spiritual growth. I wouldn't write one of those, even if I could. Though, I do hope that, even in small ways, you can see parts of yourself in my story, as nuanced as it is. I hope that this book serves as a counterpoint if you've been hurt by a religious institution or have encountered messages that queer and trans folks don't need, care about or belong in faith-based or spiritual communities. As strange and wonderfully weird as my life has been, I hope you come away feeling connected.

Books are a funny form of communication. I'm so used to the temporality of the Internet: writing blogs that are out in a day, writing posts that get liked, shared, and then buried in my page, or hopping on an IG live to share my thoughts for the week, direct from me to you. As far as my own spiritual journey goes, I don't know where I'll be by the time you're reading this. I'm currently invested in energy work, certified in Reiki II, and mix spiritual coaching with energy healing and tarot spreads alongside running Kinky Confessionals, where I hold space and share resources and positive affirmations for LGBTQ+ folks who hold shame about their desires. This journey is ongoing, and I am committed to seeing where it takes me.

I can hear my publisher saying, "Ok, but where are the jokes in this section? Can we add something quippy about Jesus here?" I don't want to lead y'all astray and be too serious as we close this thing up. Not after you've been with me for this long. Like I said, this isn't a how-to, and I'm not here to put a bow on all this work and put it under a Christmas tree.

But it is an offering, an approach to openness when embarking on your own spiritual journey. It's a reminder that our spiritual centers aren't a solid and unchanging foundation. They are learning centers, ever-evolving and with space for all that calls to our inner selves and brings us joy.

157

So my last offering for you is this reflection:

> What is bringing you joy right now?
> What is weighing on you?
> What is no longer serving you?
>
> Where is your energy going?
>
>> <u>Think</u>
>> connections and relationships, both
>> professional and personal, work
>> tasks, worrying, planning, thinking,
>> building, making, moving
>
> Are you getting back what you're
> putting in energetically?

> When was the last time that you laughed so hard
> that it was the only thing you were doing? Who
> was there? What sparked that release? How
> can you make more time for that feeling?
>
> Which parts of your day or your week do
> you look forward to the most, and which
> are you low-key *(or high-key)* dreading?
>
> When was the last time you were in
> nature? Which natural settings spark your
> deepest breaths, your easiest stillness?
>
> What would you do with your time if you had no
> restrictions *(time, money, resources, people, etc.)*?
> So much of our journey involves figuring out
> what we truly want, and being brave enough
> to write it down, say it out loud, and move
> towards it. Your spiritual journey and your life
> path is ever-evolving.

This book is simply an offering. What you do with it is up to you.

Wishing you abundance, patience, and radiant queer joy on your journey, wherever it takes you.

—Bex

Acknowledgements

It's no exaggeration to say that this book would not be in your hands and out in the world without the support, encouragement, and expertise of my publisher and "book doula," Lou Barrett. When she first approached me with this possibility, I had no idea what a journey I was signing up for, emotionally and mentally. Through her thoughtful questions, heart-felt affirmations, and efficient pacing, we were able to watch this book grow from a skeleton of ideas into the full-fledged book baby that it is today. For that, and for our connection, I am ever-grateful.

I hold so much appreciation for the many creative and brilliant beings who invested their time, energy, and talents to bring this once-Google-Doc to life. Many thanks to Ashley King, who spiritually envisioned and created the cover and layout, Jessi Knox who actually pulled tarot cards to direct the illustrations, and Cordelia Eddy, my editor, who was able to advocate for my readers and seamlessly enhance my writing while maintaining my message. To our focus group volunteers and Patreon members and followers of House Of Our Queer, thank you for being on this journey from the start and for being the spiritual community I was hoping to build.

It only seems fitting to acknowledge my gratitude for the late College of New Rochelle, my very first home away from home and the mysterious donor and universal life forces that brought me there. I raise my glass to my eternal professors, Dr. Amy Bass and Dr. Nick Smart, my first teachers in critical thinking and questioning, who have been supportive mentors long beyond graduation. To my girlfriend, Cheryna, butch babe of my dreams, thank you for everything; for helping me to grow this seed of spiritual support from wonderings over long hikes and lots of questions, for being my behind-the-scenes Queer Church tech helper, and for encouraging my winding passions, wherever they lead.

As you may tell from reading this book, I would not be who I am or doing any of this work without my connections and family in the queer community, in the Bay and Brooklyn.

My heart and my joy are always abundant thanks to you. I am able to continue this work thanks to the energy and connection from my queer, spiritual community and growing network, including my Shine Your Light soul siblings, *Nourish* family, and badass witches everywhere.

Thank you to my bio fam, especially my mom and dad. Thank you for your bravery to be together, to grow our family, and to support me through the journey of it all. I hope you can tell from this book how much I appreciate you and the many ways that you continue to learn with me in this lifetime.

Finally, I'd like to send a line of appreciation to my tiny, younger self for surviving and to my adult self for facing all of the feels that came up while writing. I honor all of the queer spiritual icons and inspirations named in this book, especially Risa Dickens and Amy Torok from *Missing Witches* for writing the intro.

My deep gratitude to all of the ancestors, spirits, goddexes, and magic makers guiding me to and through this continual work, wherever it leads.

About Bex Mui

Bex Mui is a biracial, queer, lesbian, cis femme organizer and consultant committed to the work of LGBTQ+ affirmation at the intersections of education, spirituality, and sexual and mental wellness.

As a queer spiritual organizer, Bex believes that a spiritually grounded approach to the work of LGBTQ+ advocacy is increasingly needed, as well as an expansive, shame-free. spiritually-grounded approach to sexuality. Bex created the online class, "Decolonizing Gender," for the Antiracist Educator Institute, and has presented on anti-racist, LGBTQ-centered advocacy at the local, state, and national level. You can find out more about Bex on her website at BexMui.com.